Business Tips

About the author

Karel de Laat completed his bachelor's and master's degrees in psychology and his doctorate in history in Australia. He worked as an organizational psychologist for forty years, specializing in organization and career development. During this time he featured in newspapers and on radio providing practical advice on how to achieve personal and business success, as well as presenting seminars on a wide range of business and career development subjects. In his spare time, Karel served in the Royal Australian Naval Reserve for thirty years, attaining the rank of Rear-Admiral. He now devotes his time to mentoring, consulting, public speaking and writing. His other books include *Hints for Personal Success.*

About the book

Business Tips is full of examples of how to use the experience of others to make your life more rewarding. Psychologist Karel de Laat has provided advice to owners and managers of large businesses and to their many employees. In his work, he collected numerous anecdotes and used them to motivate and guide his clients. Karel believes that everyone has a unique role to play in the world, focusing on those with whom we live, work and relax. We can all experience life to the full, even though we do not get the same publicity as the people we may see presented to us in the media every day. The key to realizing our personal and business success is taking control of our lives, not living in the shadow of public opinion. Karel's anecdotes show in a practical way how each of us can achieve the personal and business success we want or make the dramatic step to realizing we already have it right in front of us and that you just have not been able to see or grasp it yet.

The more power, resources and technology a manager has, the better the chances of creating something successful and meaningful. Unfortunately, the ego distortion and lack of perspective that often goes with this power has resulted in some of the most unsuccessful and meaningless ventures in history.

The first sign of impending disaster is when members of the management team value their own opinions and self importance above the importance of the venture itself.

The second sign is when they start to treat members of the wider team as lesser contributors to the success of the enterprise.

When you see these signs, head elsewhere as fast as you can.

Published by de Laat & Co
PO Box 9 Ferny Hills Distribution Centre
Brisbane QLD Australia 4055
www.delaatco.com

The preferred citation for this book is

FK de Laat, *Business Tips*, de Laat & Co, Brisbane, 2015.

Author: Karel de Laat
Title: Business Tips/Karel de Laat
ISBN: 978-0-9872878-1-6
Subjects: psychology, philosophy, business

Business Tips

Karel de Laat

de Laat & Co

Contents

Introduction

Being a success in business requires a wide range of skills including leadership, management, selling and customer service plus the motivation to apply and keep developing your skills in the face of some pretty trying situations.

Most of all, to really succeed, you need the ability to cope with a wide variety of circumstances with a large slice of common sense and a well developed personal business philosophy.

Over the years I have published a variety of business articles, which I now present to you in this book as Business Tips. Business is a very personal thing and to enjoy it you need to do it on your own terms.

The various case studies, principles and exercises in this book are organized to help you explore your talents and let you apply them in business in the most efficient way.

In considering these thoughts I hope you will compare them to your own and use the resulting combination of ideas to make your business life better.

You can just browse anywhere you like, but I believe that noting any thoughts that you have or action that you plan to take as you are reading is the best way to turn your intentions into actions. For this reason, I have included sections for notes throughout the book, with the first example on the next page asking you why you are reading this book at all.

In using the ideas I hope they help you to achieve what you define as personal and business success.

Best wishes,

Karel de Laat

What do I want to achieve by reading Business Tips?

_____

_____

_____

_____

_____

_____

_____

_____

_____

_____

_____

_____

_____

_____

_____

_____

_____

_____

Business Tips

Age does not weary them

Legislation has been introduced to prevent discrimination in employment on a range of characteristics over the years. One of the most significant of these is age. The aim of the legislation is to prevent decisions being made in employment matters on grounds that are irrelevant to the likely work performance of the individual, young or old.

Unfortunately, age remains one of the characteristics most difficult to combat as a source of discrimination. So many things hinge on age throughout an individual's life that it is difficult not to use age information in a comparative way. In newspapers for example, it was and in some places still is customary to include an individual's age with their name under their photograph when this serves no useful purpose whatever.

One of the most concerning issues in age discrimination is that business not just the individual misses out on a great opportunity. In speaking recently to a forty-eight year old job candidate, I found him to be very frustrated purely by this age discrimination factor.

This person was extremely well presented, energetic, innovative and had a range of very good skills in industrial sales that I knew were much sought after and much needed in a variety of industries.

'I found myself being interviewed by sales managers under 30' he told me 'and I could see in their eyes the thought "Why doesn't this old guy just retire and get out of the way?", but most of the time though I do not even get an interview'.

There are organizations that recognize the value of extensive experience as well as the fact that extensive experience cannot be obtained in a short period of time. One of my clients recently stipulated the need for a person over 40 to fill a particular management job vacancy.

Even this statement was, of course, a breach of the legislation. What they really meant was that they required someone with a minimum of 15 years management experience. Nevertheless, the outcome was the same and twenty years of sound management experience was brought into play in an organization that will benefit greatly from acquiring someone with this level of skill.

Of course, I can hear you thinking 'What if those 20 years is just the same year 20 times?' and yes you are right, putting numbers to anything can be a trap.

Nevertheless, business can benefit greatly from correctly applying the substantial experience that more senior job candidates can bring into the organization.

To get this benefit, business managers and owners need to recognize where this experience can be used. They also need the wisdom and courage to go against a still prevailing wind that blows in favor of youth and assumed vitality, even if this is not part of the job specification (which it might be of course).

In the final analysis, the key issue must be the skills required for the job and a selection process based on job relevant criteria.

Ambitious employees a plus

Conducting a series of career development workshops for the employees of a large organization recently, reminded me how personal drive and ambition can run hand in hand with corporate success. Quite contrary to being divisive, the development of ambition in a large number of employees gives them a common base to work from in achieving the organization's goals.

Too often, employees' have lived in fear of being so outspoken that they attracted the 'wrong' attention and the organization suffered because some of the best ideas come out of an urgent and sometimes conflicting environment. With the encouragement of striving for individual success and individual reward, the organization builds the foundation of a strong and creative team.

The secret to staying away from the negative aspects of so much naked ambition is ensuring that communication within the organization is honest and widespread. One good way of doing this is publicizing (without too much rah rah) the achievements, as they occur, of each and every member of the team. Thus reinforcing the positive nature of the competitive environment and ensuring that the right people get the publicity.

In times gone by, some organizations avoided developing employees because they did not want to be the training ground for their competitors or lose valuable employees who became "too" ambitious. Fortunately, a lot of this thinking has disappeared. These organizations were the losers as much as their employees.

If you build a fiercely competitive team, in which all members thrive on the successes of every member, your organization will grow to provide every reward your ambitious employees are seeking.

Are they motivated to change

Many years ago I conducted an exercise with seventeen managers and gave them a special test that I used to assess how motivated they were towards a management career as opposed to continuing to specialize in operations.

Significantly, the seventeen people at this conference were already managers and this was a special management development program oriented towards strategic planning. I had been asked to do some revision on the general principles of management and management commitment as an introduction to the main theme of the conference, which was strategic planning and budgets.

It was fascinating that the testing process revealed that only two of the seventeen managers had any real interest in management. Further investigation in a seminar/discussion session revealed that fifteen of these managers had taken on management roles simply because it was the only way they could get a promotion and more money.

In this highly technical company, all of these managers had a technical background and far preferred to do their technical work rather than the much more onerous work of managing people. Nevertheless, they had all accepted the responsibility of managing others, which they really did not like doing.

Very recently, I struck an identical situation where people in management positions did not have the skills to be there and did not want to be there. In this case, the senior management of the organization had not taken account of the motivation of the individuals to a management career (or not).

Unfortunately, the situation from the original example still applied and going into management for these people was the only way to get a promotion and hence more money.

So what can be done about this dilemma? Certainly, the overall health of the business would be much better served by identifying people who wanted to be managers, providing them with the skills and finding a way to compensate those who were good at and wanted to stay with technical careers.

Unfortunately, western society has an obsession with the goal of being a manager. This does not seem to be changing as more and more business management courses are created. One person even mentioned to me recently about a one day Master of Business Administration course that could be done by video.

Where does it all end? This is a decision to be made by senior managers in organizations. They need to take rapid action to ensure that management study is not undertaken by the wrong people for the wrong reasons.

Also, when people present with management qualifications but without the skills or motivation to be managers, they should ensure that these people are counseled to continue their career in a technical area.

The process of counseling people away from a management career that will not suit them is not easy. Also, many managers who should be doing the counseling are the people who have moved into management without the right skills or motivation so the problem is a constantly compounding one.

In addition, business management schools are sales oriented and can be expected to accept and encourage any person with the time and money to do their courses.

Hopefully, the market forces of sound management will drive the quest for the recognition of the people who want to be managers for the right reasons. Only in this way will there be any improvement in overall long term business quality.

What are my own motivations to change? Are they the right ones?

_____

_____

_____

_____

_____

_____

_____

_____

_____

_____

_____

_____

_____

_____

_____

_____

_____

Bad tourism merchandising

In travelling to a function recently, I experienced a not-so- joyous taxi cab ride through an inner city area.

The cab itself had set the mood because it was dirty, smelly and in a very poor state of repair. Pieces were falling off the seat, the speaker from the radio was hanging out of the bottom of the dashboard and so on.

As we drove through what was once an inner city industrial area, but was supposed to be now developing as an inner city tourist area, I was assailed by litter, graffiti and various forms of industrial junk collecting in and near a variety of premises.

We have to ask ourselves in presenting an image like this for tourists, what would they think of this tourism merchandising?

It is all very well to talk about developing a tourism industry that does not destroy the natural quality of our environment. However, who are we to police this circumstance if we cannot maintain a basic standard ourselves?

I have spoken previously about the need for public utilities that function on a seven day a week twenty-four hour a day basis, ensuring that the minimum standards of city hygiene, safety and general orderliness are maintained. It certainly seems that some local action is required to get that sort of commitment.

I read with great interest recently of groups of citizens being formed to patrol areas of their city to identify problem spots in terms of security lighting etc.

This reminded me of many years ago working in a large enterprise where an appointed architect and assistant would inspect the premises daily to ensure that the integrity of a master plan had not been violated. This organization maintained an outstanding physical environment for its four million visitors per year whilst continuing to operate as a productive entity.

The issue in this type of circumstance seems to be directly related to a quality attitude. Appropriate legislation, planned preventive maintenance and a vision that can be put into effect, are all key elements in preventing the types of problems mentioned here.

Regrettably, the gloss associated with public relations often obscures the reality of what happens on a day-to-day basis on the streets. Only action by the people who are involved can bring attention to the problems and ensure that the appropriate resources are allocated.

The outcome for all concerned will be a more pleasant, safer city for residents and tourists alike.

Baseball bat management

With all the advances in human resource management and constant discussion about new techniques, one does not expect to hear stories about large companies treating their employees poorly.

No matter how often I am surprised by these stories, I am still disappointed when I hear about companies that are household names allowing their managers to treat employees of long standing in a manner that is just totally inconsistent with the image that they present.

Recently, I had cause to counsel two employees who had been retrenched from a large organization. They advised me of a situation of another employee who had been retrenched just months short of retirement after over 20 years service, in a manner that showed utter disregard for her contribution to the company.

As the person that I was meeting with said: 'What was done was not the issue, because the person's rights were respected - it was how it was done'. He then went on to give a very good re-enactment of someone with a baseball bat hitting someone else right behind the ear.

Apparently this person, although very close to retirement, was told that her job was to be made redundant. Apparently, there was a heavy emphasis at the conclusion of this person's career that really her contribution to the company had not been all that it could have been.

This inference was made despite this person being officially rated as one of the most competent people in the organization over many years. In addition, she had performed any task that had been required of her and had been totally committed to the company throughout.

It seems that these situations just do not get better.

So where does this leave us all from a business point of view? To me it confirms once again that for a company to have a heart, it must have managers that are good managers of people.

There needs to be only one break in this succession of people who are good people managers for the company to become totally heartless with the result that one episode in a person's career is poorly managed and a career ruined.

It seems that the organization that has been discussed here is having a hard time and things are getting worse. However, it seems from the details available, that the hard times are of the organization's own making.

The senior executives are treating the company as a collection of objects, not as a living, breathing enterprise employing many thousands of people. This is an attitude they will regret, but probably will never realize or admit its full significance.

Benchmarking benefits

Maintaining a go forward attitude is a problem for all of us at times and businesses are no exception.

Over the past few years more and more people are turning to benchmarking to help get motivated to achieve better performance.

Benchmarking is essentially about developing a set of measures to assess your business performance. So what is the big deal about that? Isn't profit enough to show you how you are performing?

The key to benchmarking is the possibilities it offers to work out particular measures that apply to your business in some unique way.

In reality, most people trade off the benefits of uniqueness for the benefit of sharing information within their industry or some other group, which allows the more economical development and maintenance of better data.

Even the smallest business, however, can work out the Key Results Areas (KRAs) that best predict their eventual profit/success on an ongoing basis and use these tools on a daily weekly or monthly basis to manage activities.

An example of a classic KRA is customer service, but it is not enough to have some vague idea of how you treated your customer each day. You must measure customer service using accurate and reliable tools and therein lays the difficulty.

The design of useful measures is the tricky part of Benchmarking and you are best served to work with an industry association or similar organization when you have made the philosophical breakthrough to accepting external measurement as a business management aid.

Beware of subliminal messages

Many organizations have been putting together fairly complex and expensive promotional material, but failing to achieve their goals.

Several reasons for this became abundantly clear to me recently after receiving a follow up call to a promotional newsletter from a marketing organization.

I did recall receiving the promotional news leaflet with a handwritten note signed with an individual's initials. I still do not know if the hand writing was original or printed but it certainly struck me as being original at the time.

I thought that it had been sent by one of my clients and I remember being quite surprised at the very poor quality of the leaflet. Poor quality was not characteristic of this particular client and the poor quality reproduction and poor quality content made me wonder why she had sent the information at all.

Before I had an opportunity to speak to this client again, a representative of the marketing organization had called to follow up on the personal note from the company that had sent the leaflet.

Apparently, this company was in the business of advising on sales and marketing strategies and the follow up call was to determine whether I would like to subscribe to their leaflet on sales and marketing.

I explained to the caller that the leaflet had ended up in the waste paper basket because I was thoroughly unimpressed by what appeared to be a photocopy of a photocopy of a photocopy. While the content was suppose to promote in depth knowledge of sales and marketing topics on the part of the consultant (I did not agree with the philosophies), the presentation certainly showed a total lack of any skill in presenting a quality message to the prospective customer.

I explained my views to the caller who, to her credit, grasped the great difficulty she would have in recovering the situation and politely terminated the discussion. This made me think: "How often do companies intend to send one message but send another?"

The answer was not long in coming because, as I drove home early that evening, I noticed a sign on top of a multi-storey building in Brisbane's version of Silicon Valley. It showed the name of a well known computer company in brightly lit red letters shining like a beacon visible for many kilometers.

I assumed that this very large sign was designed to indicate that this was a company of substance, quality and importance. The only problem was that one of the letters in the sign was flickering on and off like a fluorescent bulb that could not quite make up its mind whether it had any energy left. Worse still, it was still flickering a week later.

In the computer business, one thing you certainly want to convey to your customers is that you are reliable. Unfortunately for this company, in our society you cannot get much more unreliable than a faulty light bulb.

Image consultants are doing a roaring trade at the moment telling executives that it is no good sprouting forth a message of quality, if your personal appearance presents a 'don't care' attitude. In business, it is important to apply this same principle to every avenue of marketing, sales, customer service and public relations. Make sure the customer gets the right message in every way.

Career change dilemma

A colleague, whom I had not seen for many years, was speaking about the difficulty of changing careers when a fair degree of progress had already been made in one area. This is not an uncommon dilemma.

In his particular case, he wanted to change from one industry area to another and was experiencing great difficulty in gaining the confidence of the senior executives who interviewed him during the selection process.

He was keen to show prospective employers that he had the potential to perform as well in this new area as he had been performing in his previous role. As he said "Everyone nodded their heads, but nobody offered me a job."

He said that his problem was shared by many friends who had found that the career that they thought would be theirs for life had lost its appeal or challenge and left them wanting to do something new.

As well as wanting to convince an employer in a new industry of their merit, many of these executives did not know what else they were suited to.

It would be easy to say that going to your local career counselor would give you a quick and painless solution. Unfortunately, this aspect of life is no simpler than any other.

The assessment itself should be relatively painless if it is conducted by a qualified Organizational Psychologist with a business background, but the challenge that will be set in making the decision to change will be fearsome.

Strong words you will no doubt think. However, movement out of familiar territory is always more intimidating than thinking about it.

The important thing about the decision to get professional direction in relation to career counseling is the clear signal to yourself that you have decided to get serious. Having made this decision, there is a lot of pressure on you to live up to your dreams by making the necessary effort.

Almost inevitably, the psychological assessment accompanying your career counseling session will raise challenging thoughts about perceptions you had about important aspects of your ability, employment interest or aptitude, personality and overall career history.

Dealing with these challenges is the key part of the process of deciding that it is time to get serious about a career change. Meeting this challenge begins during the counseling process where it is very important to convince yourself of the value of some very simple principles of how to manage this process.

First, you have chosen to be there and you are the customer. For that reason, you are in charge of the situation and should be responsible for understanding what is going on and ensuring that you are satisfied with the result.

Second, the psychologist is there to help you and should be perceived and treated as a specialist resource that needs clear input from you on your needs. It is vital to be open at all times in the process to get full benefit from the exercise you have initiated.

Third, you must realize that many tests are completely subjective. The answers you give make up the result you get. If you 'fudge' the answers, you are only wasting an opportunity to use a system designed to help you.

Finally, psychology is a very inexact science at the best of times, but in psychological testing it is at its least exact in some areas of personality and vocational testing.

You must use reality testing in conjunction with the psychologist to get the real benefit from the information you are given, but this does not mean that you should reject unpalatable information because it lacks the clarity you were hoping for. Even uncertain information is a beginning for you in the career planning process.

So if you are in a dilemma with respect to career decision making, do seek professional assistance, but make sure you do not abdicate your personal responsibility.

Remember, the interior decorator has no ownership of your house just because you let them help you choose the direction you take. The organizational psychologist who advises you on your career options is no different.

Change with the times

Sadly, I have been counseling and advising many more individuals whose businesses are not going well.

Essentially they are small business people and there is often a common reason for their demise.

I have often spoken about resistance to change. Nowhere is resistance to change more telling than in the fortunes of a small business.

In some cases, I have told small business operators of the need to diversify or totally change their product or service, because of a universally contracting market.

Many times, they are unable to take and implement the advice I give because of their total commitment to the past.

They have been successful with their product or service for many years and just will not accept that the market will never revive.

Saddest of all, these people cling to their belief right through total bankruptcy and blame all manner of things other than their own resistance to change.

One of the most important characteristics that any business person can have is the ability to recognize the need for change.

Change in products, change in skills and change driven by customer tastes are all areas in which successful business people anticipate and act upon potential negative influences on their activities.

Unfortunately, the capacity to recognize, work with, and capitalize on change seems to be difficult to acquire.

Some strategies that may assist with keeping an open mind to change include:-

1.   Attendance at general business rather than industry specific seminars.
2.   Getting input from a diverse range of employees within the organization.
3.   Observing objectively the strategies and fortunes of competitors.
4.   Following closely the trends in markets which have traditionally been an indicator of future activities in your own market.
5,   Studying success in all industries, not just your own.

It is extremely difficult to be prescriptive about something that decides the fortune of so many businesses, but the important aspect of recognizing inflexibility on your own part will go a long way towards ensuring that you do not become a victim of the well know "Dinosaur Syndrome".

Collect that money

Cash flow is the name of the game you will hear so many people say about success in business. I had this dramatically brought home to me on an assignment where I was brought in extremely late in the piece to see how a business might be saved.

One of the most frightening things I discovered about this 'successful' business, with numerous design awards and a very high quality product range, was the large amount of money it was owed by its customers.

The Managing Director of the firm told me that he had personally been trying to collect various accounts for months, but without success. He told me that in all cases, the customers were not happy with the work.

Upon investigating a number of these accounts, I found that the customers were in fact not happy with a part of the work. One classic case involved an invoice of over $100,000, where the unsatisfactory work accounted for approximately $2,000 of the total invoice.

With my client's company literally facing bankruptcy, immediate action was required.

I agreed with the customer that if I could collect the amount that was not contested, $98000.00, at 9.00 the next morning and they could keep the $2,000. The following morning I collected the money and started the process of reducing the company's debt and, hopefully, getting its cash flow back on track.

The story with other customers was similar. Hundreds of thousands of dollars were being held up because trade staff had not returned to examine faults that had amounted to only 1% of the work. This was not a time to argue about who was right and who was wrong. The business needed money so concessions needed to be made for cash.

The key factor in this situation was the failure to collect accounts promptly and effectively. The accountant for the firm felt it was beneath him to call people to ask for money, and he had not allocated the work to a person skilled in the area.

The Managing Director at the latter stages took the responsibility himself but was totally ineffective through lack of experience.

In addition, this was the first time the company had accepted very large construction contracts where people did not just pay their accounts, you had to collect.. He had never had to chase money in large amounts before because he had worked with a few loyal customers.

A few simple points, followed religiously, could have saved this company. They are:

1. Analyze your prospective customers and be sure that you have a credit policy.
2. Monitor credit levels and payments very carefully.
3. Act quickly but carefully to collect doubtful accounts.
4. If you do not have the skill to do the job, get someone who has.

Above all else, remember that experience is the key to this tough end of business.

Constructive response will win the day

On one occasion, I wrote a newspaper column criticizing the administration of junior rowing in my district.

I was delighted to be approached by the senior administrators from the sport, who genuinely wanted to get as much information from me as possible, to incorporate into their plans for improvement.

In my view, this response to criticism is the only way to go. It is a clear reflection of an open minded and constructive attitude to the improvement of individual and group performance.

One of the greatest difficulties we have in improving our own performance is keeping an open mind about constructive criticism. We speak about it so often as being essential to the development of a wide range of group activities, but how often do people practice what they preach?

Too many people throw the baby out with the bath water and adopt a totally defensive attitude. This is particularly unfortunate because it inhibits personal growth and future performance.

So how can we ensure that we can get the benefit of constructive criticism without being defensive?

One of the first things that must be included in our portfolio of skills is the ability to be objective. This is not easy, but I believe that objectivity is very often directly proportional to a person's professionalism.

Second, one has to retain the view that any person who is critical, does this with the clear intention of being helpful to the person or activity that they are criticizing. This is very difficult, but one has to retain the view that if a person takes the trouble to be critical, it is because they care and wish to see things change for the better.

Third, one has to truly believe the very old saying that: "Nobody is perfect". In the same vein, it follows that everybody is imperfect and will always be subject to criticism. Once you accept that this is a natural state, criticism is something that you welcome and use as a tool to improve your performance.

Unfortunately, these three principles sound great until you are the subject of the criticism. From there, the challenge is to have big shoulders upon which to rest that very open mind. Good luck! If you are able to achieve that objectivity, empathy and open-minded approach, you are destined to make big improvements in your performance.

Continuous improvement

CIP or Continuous Improvement Program is a basic term these days in management jargon, but a lot of people are still either skeptical or afraid. A lot of trendy management ideas might deserve a wide berth, but this is not one of them.

In the simplest terms, continuous improvement is about never giving up the effort(and it is an effort) to bring a fresh approach to your business in every area in the search for ways to achieve better performance.

We all like our comforts at some time, but a CIP says that, while you may have rest days, you will never be complacent about how your business operates and the job of setting ever more challenging goals.

The basic preparation in installing of a Continuous Improvement Program involves a

- standard upon which to base the assessment of you improvement, and
- a well thought out measure or set of measures that is universally understood by the members of the organization that requires painstaking work, but sets an undeniable standard for all to focus on.

But beware! The implementation and failure of any improvement is worse than no program at all.

Good intentions and no follow through by the famous 'gunners', who are gunner do this and gunner do that and eventually do nothing but crush the spirit of the most devoted employee.

So it is worth doing, but do it right or do not do it at all.

Cook the talk

It was great visiting a new riverside restaurant recently, because of the great ambience created by the river at night, the design of the premises and the very impressive sounding menu. Unfortunately, it turned out to be a re-run of a similar experience in Paris some years ago.

We found ourselves in the University quarter outside the Sorbonne with an appetite which said 'Let's do the tourist thing and have a national dish'. On the menu the food sounded great, but on the plate and in the mouth and tummy it was more than a little ordinary.

So it was with our home grown product. The menu read brilliantly and the whole experience was shaping to be a night to remember, but something was missing. The food was ordinary. Everything was there. It was not bad food by any means, but there was no magic - and the atmosphere promised magic.

All businesses should aim for magic, but these days the outer trappings of magic are too easy to find in a book. The end result can be that the appearance of something special is achieved, but the substance is missing. Often this gets you into the situation where things go well for a while, but then there is no repeat business, the business does not build and you fail.

No one wants to see anyone fail, especially when so much has been done right, but this is an area where solutions are very difficult to prescribe. The magic is so often in the person who owns the business and that talent is either there or not. The best backup strategy has to be that, if you can see that something is missing, you find someone you know has got the talent and get them to help you, but beware of imposters.

The most important thing is to realize that the key to success is having the full package. The trimmings and the substance have to blend together and be dressed up to provide the final solution that people flock to - the magical experience.

Cool, calm and a classic

I was fortunate to be on the spot recently when a customer service representative at a large retail store was put on the spot. She ignored a customer who had been waiting for some time and attended to a query from another staff member.

However, when the customer indicated his displeasure she gave a classic response and the situation did not even look like getting out of hand.

The first thing she did was follow the golden rule of handling complaints - KEEP CALM. She did not need to GET THE FACTS because she was well aware of her mistake.

What she clearly knew was to NOT TAKE THE COMPLAINT PERSONALLY, thereby ensuring that there could never be any conflict. In a totally genuine manner she indicated her regret at failing to see the customer and moved on quickly and efficiently to provide the service that was required.

It is so simple to diffuse potentially difficult situations, if you are trained to maintain a cool, calm and professional approach. Yet so many people who deal with the public are quick to take personally offense.

An easy way to get a fresh perspective on the situation is to think about the limited nature of your relationship with customers. They do not know you, so how could they possibly dislike you. Just remember, all anyone is looking for is fair and efficient service. Exactly the type of service you would like if you were in their shoes is all they want.

If things get off the rails, just get them back on again as fast and politely as possible and keep the customer informed at all times. It is that simple.

Corporate chaos

You would be excused for believing that the planning and implementation at major sporting events would be outstanding with everybody vying for our entertainment dollar. However, it seems that we just cannot seem to learn the simplest lessons.

At a recent sporting event I was fortunate enough to enjoy a great game from the comfort of a corporate box. Unfortunately, the experience was not complemented by great service. On its own, the poor service would not have been a problem, but nobody seemed to realize the power of a little advance warning of impending deprivation.

Hey, with the home side absolutely killing the opposition(on the scoreboard I mean), who cares about the food being an hour late. Unless you are expecting it of course and decide to interrupt your fun to check what is going on. Still not a major problem though was my thought. Still, it is amazing how even the best day can have the edge taken off it by the almost inevitable false promise - "It will be right there". Especially when right there is another 20 minute delay on top of the hour already gone by.

Enough complaining! How do you fix it? Easy! Either hire experienced staff or train them before you send them out into the fray. The corners you cut now are the ones that come back to haunt you. Maybe not this week, or this year if you are the flavor of the month, but certainly next year when those corporate box holders ask their customers - Who will we go with, the x or the y?

Finally, what about the poor staff who spend their lives making excuses for a botch up that is not their fault? Who can blame them for losing a bit of their zip. Although, it still amazes me how good people keep on keeping on even under the most atrocious conditions. Do not let it happen to you! By the time this crowd get the message from the odd "Did you have a good time brochure?" they handed out it will be all too late.

Customer service is still the decider

In speaking recently to a state manager with more than 15 years experience in his current organization and a lifetime in his industry, I was delighted to have the value of customer service so convincingly confirmed.

This particular person was lamenting a total head office change of direction as a result of which the focus was being taken away from the customer interface and returned very squarely to the analysis of data by senior managers well removed from all branch activity.

It was most interesting that this particular individual had long held the view that, in his competitive industry where all suppliers had basically the same products being distributed through identical channels, the relationship with the customer was what provided the opportunity to be more competitive.

Certainly, no one could afford to be 'off the pace with their pricing he said, but neither would outright price cutting bring customers flocking to the door.

From an organizational point of view, this particular manager emphasized the responsibility to correctly manage stock availability as being of paramount importance.

This is noteworthy, as I have seen this subject raised elsewhere in strategic planning sessions as a high priority strategy for success, particularly for organizations supplying a wide range of products.

From a personal point of view, this manager felt that the customer relationship was the key, with the main emphasis being on the willingness and capacity to go the extra distance, make the extra phone call or the carry out the extra visit to ensure that the customer was happy.

It is interesting that even for companies that pride themselves on installing elaborate customer service systems the simple criteria of having stock available and delivering it on time is often not satisfied at even a fifty percent level.

The rules for success are simple. Following the rules is much more difficult. There is a definite need to personalize the process of goal setting for customer satisfaction. If members of the organization do not see how customer service relates to their job, they will do nothing to contribute to it.

While customer service remains an abstract concept the business manager can expect little improvement.

Customer service wins

Very rarely did I name any organization in my newspaper column, good or bad, but on one occasion I made an exception.

I dropped off two watches to have the batteries replaced to a local watchmaker where I had experienced excellent service in the past.

On this occasion, the situation was no different with the staff all being very friendly. However, the stand out and stand up act was the watchmaker himself.

Sitting behind the watch repair counter, he had a big smile on his face and kept on wise cracking and just generally enjoying his work. But does it do any good for his business you ask?

It certainly does. I came back from doing some shopping and, contrary to promises and expectations he had not yet started on my battery replacement job.

I was in a hurry because I was helping to organize a function. Despite this and the fact that I had a large platter of cold food that was going to start getting warm, I did not feel the slightest niggle.

I just started happily chatting to the watchmaker, who suggested that I could take my armful of supplies to the car and the work would be ready by the time I got back.

Totally happy (even though I was using up extra time), I wandered off to the car, deposited my shopping, made a telephone call and went back to find my watches ready and waiting.

The circumstances in this situation were no different than on many other occasions when I have experienced poor customer service and used the example to illustrate what not to do. So what was so different about this situation.

According to the watchmaker (who I found out owned the business), 'most watchmakers are just too stuffy and take themselves too seriously'. For this reason he had decided to do the opposite as much as he was able. He created a friendly chatty atmosphere with a very personal approach, while still doing the job properly. On top of all this, the prices were competitive.

To me this is the classic example of how great customer rapport can overcome minor frustrations with customers that in other circumstances might blow up into a major negative and result in the loss of future business. For this reason, I had no hesitation in naming this business in my newspaper column (something I rarely did).

Develop computer literacy

In these days where computers are everywhere and technology is developing at such a rapid rate, it is surprising that many business people are still not computer literate.

I met recently with a senior executive, who felt that he was particularly well informed because he had taken time out to develop computing skills and hire professional advisors.

Upon investigating the state of computing in his organization, however, it was very clear to me that the whole system was a mish-mash of uncoordinated hardware and software.

If a large organization which employs computer professionals has a poorly coordinated and ineffective computer strategy, how can mere mortals cope?.

The reality is that the more computer literacy and computer awareness <u>every member of the organization</u> has, the more successful the computer strategy will be.

It is not sufficient to allow the computer strategy to be driven by the specialist. Information management is the realm of every single employee.

Certainly, expert decisions that require weeks or months of research need to be informed by a well qualified specialist in the area. But there is no reason why all employees cannot be given formal computer literacy instruction so that they are aware of the most basic elements of the computer world.

One particular test that I have always used in the selection of hardware and software is exceedingly simple. It surprises me how so many people still ignore this basic principle.

Any person who is thinking of buying a particular item of computer hardware or software should ask the computer salesperson or consultant: 'Where can you show me this item being used by someone else successfully for the same purpose for which I wish to purchase it?'.

So many people buy an item, not just in the computer area where it is particularly critical, where they do not do their research to ensure that it is capable of performing the functions that they need.

In the computer area where the opportunity to make mistakes is multiplied by thousands or millions, you cannot afford to experiment or, as so many people proudly tell me, 'be the first in the area'. In computing, being the first in the area means that you are on a boat far out at sea with no support and no way of getting to safety if something goes wrong. This is a very dangerous place to be.

To carry the ship analogy on, if your engine fails, you will float away. It is no good pulling out the oars because it will have no impact whatever. I have seen situations where a large computer system failed to perform and the whole works system had to be offloaded onto a whole range of smaller systems. This was expensive and almost sent the company to the wall.

So if you want to avoid these types of problems take the time to make yourself aware of the basics of computing as it relates to business and give your employees and team members the same training. This will lead to the sort of environment that encourages a critical and informed approach to all technological change that could save your business.

Are you prepared to do a snap review of your technology? How will you do it? What do you want to find out?

Disillusionment starts early

Often, I have given examples of the absolute tragedy of people who do not practice what they preach.

However, there is a situation even worse than failure to practice what you preach. It is called utter incompetence combined with arrogance, particularly in dealing with the young and keen.

The power of incompetence and arrogance was brought home to me with great force while watching a junior sporting event recently.

The sport was rowing which requires officials to communicate, using megaphones, with the rowers on the water. It appears that often the megaphones are very difficult to hear because they are highly directional. If the individual turns the megaphone which hangs on his (I have not seen any female officials up to this time) shoulder, it turns with him and his voice carries in that direction.

On one occasion I was appalled to hear a grown man speaking to a group of young female rowers with the sort of patronizing, demeaning tone and language that would just not be acceptable in any work setting. It seemed that the rowers were guilty of the heinous crime of not hearing the swaying megaphone.

Fascinated by this situation, I investigated other aspects of the administration of this Olympic sport at junior level. I found the situation did not improve in other areas, with officialdom generally being conducted incompetently and terribly arrogantly.

One can only wonder how people in these situations can remain ignorant of the damage they do on such a large scale to young, highly impressionable minds. Interestingly this was not the first time I had seen this behavior from professional educators.

It seems that familiarity really can breed contempt in the most inappropriate situations.

Fortunately, education has progressively been working towards a broader base. Competency based training is all about realizing that all activities which improve performance can be measured and accredited.

What a shame then that we don't have the same realization and focus on the negative impact of unstructured learning situations such as sport and hobby activities.

Because of their great level of interest, students and young people in particular probably pay much more attention to their learning processes in activities that they would feel are not at all educational.

In both work and life in general, if we provide people with role models that are counterproductive because they are examples of poor attitude and incompetence, we only deserve the poor outcomes that result.

A further problem is that the poor outcome is long-term and just not acceptable in any way as it can shape the entire future of these young people. Such activities should only be conducted by properly trained and accredited people who are assessed regularly.

Document career aspirations

It is interesting that even in a smallest business with less than 10 employees, the owner or manager is often not aware of the career aspirations of the members of the workgroup.

These smaller business operators always say that there is no need for formal performance review or documentation of individuals' career aspirations, because they know their staff so well.

It is virtually inevitable, however, that when an organization review is conducted as part of a system to document career aspirations that there are a number of surprises.

One of the greatest tragedies of business, particularly in difficult times, is the failure to use individual skills and energies effectively. So many people have much more to contribute but are just not given the opportunity.

There has certainly been a healthy trend in the area of quality management where directors and managers are forced to gain input from employees at all levels. Very often this allows the employees to express their wish to contribute more and show their capabilities.

There is a related area which hampers career development for people changing jobs. To do this successfully, managers must record openly and thoroughly the skills required now and in the future by the organization. Then, similar detailed information in relation to employee skills and aspirations can be documented and matched to current and future needs.

The end result will be optimum use of employees' abilities and improved organization performance.

It is a long standing phenomenon in the selection of new employees that preference is given to candidates with specific industry experience.

Strangely, senior managers or directors will often say that the skills required do not have to come from the particular industry for which the vacancy exists. Nevertheless, on most occasions, preference is given to a candidate of lesser ability with industry experience and better candidates are being rejected because of their lack of specific industry experience.

I consider this situation to be clear evidence of the conservatism of managers associated with a fear of taking risks. Interestingly, the risk is not associated with the selection being incorrect, but much more about being able to defend an incorrect decision by saying that the individual had industry experience, therefore the mistake can be excused.

Owners and managers need to be much more skilled in documenting the essential skills for the performance of the duties associated with their business. When they do this, they will have the confidence to select more on the basis of people's career aspirations and a general set of skills that are sufficient for a person to first survive and then thrive in a new, more challenging position.

Don't be early customers

You might wonder what quiz shows and customer service would have in common, but driving into my local garage early on a Saturday morning recently made me think how things had changed in so many areas.

Many years ago, there was a very popular quiz show with a husband and wife team advertising products for a well known petroleum company. This married couple epitomized everything to do with the blending of the sale of the product with the program. Totally unsubtle sales lines and slogans were part of the entertainment.

People in the streets used the slogans incorporating the company name in greetings, jokes and every other imaginable situation giving the company an unbeatable top of mind awareness.

These days, there appear to be smoother but less effective techniques used on game shows, with a resulting loss in advertising benefits. It also seems that events on the driveway parallel the changes in the quiz show.

Recently, I pulled into a garage at five minutes to seven in the morning, while the proprietor was opening the doors and the pumps were still locked. By the time I pulled in, the owner/attendant was behind the counter and by a very expressive shrug of the shoulders indicated to me there was no way in the world he was going to solve my petrol problems.

Reflecting back on my many years of working as a schoolboy on Saturday mornings in the local garage, I remember circumstances being very different. Customers always pulled in when we were opening the doors and the only movement of the shoulders was to increase the speed with which we took the locks off the pumps, served them petrol, cleaned their windscreen, checked their tires, checked their oil and made incredibly polite conversation during the whole process.

So where is Australian customer service these days? On its backside it seems, because the average Australian customer service worker (with some industries being a notable exception I am pleased to say) has some difficulty in getting out of their own way to satisfy customer needs.

So customers, it used to be better petrol because it was Benzol Powered, but now its better petrol if you are better prepared. Do get there on time, do be prepared to serve your own petrol, check your own tires, clean your own windscreen, check your own oil and do not expect any polite conversation.

The strategy of pushing out your costs to be borne by your customers and your suppliers is not a new one. It has worked very successfully for a whole range of companies, but where it results in a deterioration of front line customer service and comes totally into conflict with basic customer service philosophy problems will definitely arise.

In certain areas, businesses need to look carefully at this strategy to ensure that in negotiating for suppliers to do all their warehousing and organizing and aiming for customers to do all their own delivery work that they do not destroy their whole business.

While some of the older philosophies may have been expensive, it can be that they meant more to the customer relationship than was realized. Now may be the time for certain businesses to gain distinct competitive advantage by reintroducing some of the ethic of business that seemed to serve so many people so well so long ago.

By the way, for those people who so often quiz me unsuccessfully about the identity of case study companies and for those who remember Bob and Dolly Dyer, the service station mentioned in the beginning of this story is definitely not the one of quiz show fame.

Don't complain, change it

In tough times, of which there have been many recently, it is very tempting to just give up the ghost and regard it as all just being too hard. In addition, it is the time many people start thinking that external factors are to blame for their failures.

Certainly, external factors are always very important in any business situation or in any individual endeavor. However, it is surprising how many of these factors we can control if we are able to apply our efforts in the right areas.

One of the key factors in changing away from this focus on external influences is to realize that we can alter the environment if we attack it in the right way. I use the word attack on purpose because that is often the amount of effort required to achieve any result.

So how do we go about achieving the changes that we want? I will list some of my suggestions in general terms and allow you to interpret them to suit your own situation.

In the first instance, it is important to pick the areas of greatest influence in relation to your needs and determine whether or not that external influence is accessible to you. This may be the appropriate government minister or some other politician, it may be one of your major suppliers, it may be someone in your own organization or it may be the representative of some other major body in the community.

In any event, you should identify those individuals who can have the most impact on your circumstances and then develop a strategy for change to meet your needs.

Of course, one of the most important aspects of attempts to change the environment is the development of strategies which indicate clearly that these changes are not only in your interest but in the interests of the wider business community.

Influencing others to change their point of view can be difficult if they stand to suffer significantly through giving up their own stance. However, very often their point of view is held only through force of habit and ignorance of alternative strategies which are in their interest as well as yours.

Regardless of the circumstances, your argument has to be very well presented because in the area of philosophies and business ideals, logic appears to have become the weakest argument of all.

Realistically, it may be necessary to abide by rules such as "the squeaky wheel gets the most oil" and "bull dust baffles brains" in preparing a comprehensive argument to win on the day. This is definitely not my preferred option, but you have to think about what the price of failure is for you, those around you and broader community if you cannot get the business of social change that is needed.

Preparation in the form of knowing your enemy, working towards your goal, and gaining full knowledge of the enemy's strengths and weaknesses, is absolutely essential.

As stated earlier, you might feel words like "attack" and "the enemy" are a little strong in these circumstances, but if you are bleeding to death from inefficient government regulation, poor customer service or any form of biased business practice, you had better start thinking in battle terms or you and your business will go down the drain.

And finally, remember the best means of defense is attack and it is amazing how positive you become when you are actually doing something rather than just moaning about the state of play. So get out there and do your ground work, formulate a strategy, attack and you will be surprised how much better you feel. Who knows, you may even have a win!

Easygoing is OK

So many people in their own businesses seem concerned that they are just too easy going and do not have the knock them down drag them out killer instinct. My answer to that is - what a relief.

We do not need a business world populated by a human form of shark that lurks waiting to eat up any wounded individual that comes along. Sure, a competitive attitude is great and helps to keep you motivated, but there is a big difference between motivation and aggression.

Being easygoing is a long way from being a fool, but some people cannot see the difference between the two. Actually, being easygoing is part of a formula for having a long and healthy business life, provided you are smart enough to do business with just enough smarts.

To me, the easygoing astute business operator uses the formula used by the smart employee - look at the results for effort expended. If you can get fair results and keep your lifestyle balanced with health and family in good shape, no one can argue with the success of your business.

The wonderful and tragic thing about life is that success is what you think it is. This is wonderful because you control everything to do with your success and tragic because so many people do not realize this until it is too late.

So, if you are easy going, pay your bills, have the respect of your customers and make a profit, you should celebrate every day. You are one of the many people who make our honest, positive culture a worthwhile thing to pass on to the next generation.

Ego can play havoc

A business owner told me recently of an astounding incident involving atrocious customer service. Apparently this person had arranged with a media group to place a major advertising feature in conjunction with a range of other businesses.

A date had been set very quickly and was at a time that did not suit a variety of the businesses. This particular owner, realizing that time to organize ideas for advertising was particularly important, rang to advise the coordinator of the feature that an alternative day some weeks away would be preferable.

Upon calling, it transpired that the coordinator of the feature was ill, so the owners' representative took the initiative and changed the date to some weeks away.

The following day the business owner (and customer) received a highly abusive telephone call from the Features Coordinator who had returned to work. It went something along the following lines:

'How dare you change the date of the feature without consulting! me! You have made a complete fool of me in front of my colleagues! You had no right to change the date!' While the owner of the business (and customer) attempted to remain businesslike and conciliate the process, the representative of the media group (I would like to say customer service representative but exaggeration is not my forte) literally ranted and raved without taking a breath.

So how could this happen in these modern times when the philosophy of customer service is on everyone's lips and supposedly so well known? There are a number of possible answers, but the most likely is that the emotional outburst by the employee of the media group was totally unrelated to the events involved and was merely an offshoot from some personal emotional conflict.

Very often over the years I have used case studies in counseling where bizarre behavior by employees was totally related to their personal emotional difficulties and not their work. The manager's role was to ascertain the true facts of the matter. Unfortunately, the situation under discussion here has a twist which leaves little, if any, room for forgiveness.

The business owner was not the media group representative's manager. This was a supplier/customer relationship. In these situations, personal emotional difficulties have no place. The customer has no responsibility for the supplier's and the supplier's employees' personal difficulties. They have their own business to run and have little time or interest in thinking about why someone who should be giving them customer service is being highly abusive.

The bottom line is that there is an ego/personality problem here that is the responsibility of the individual's manager. If the manager does not take a more investigative and supportive role, this organization will soon be searching for new customers while being totally unaware of why they are losing business.

Engineering excellence gives the edge

The search for the secret of success goes on in so many areas. People are constantly asking - how do we create a successful product? How do we get into the export market? How do we make money?

A clear example of success in developing a skill, exporting that skill and having a successful organization was presented to me very recently.

The example featured one of Australia's leading engineering firms. I was speaking to one of their senior directors who had just come back from a long assignment overseas. He was explaining that their level of skill was at such a point that the normally arduous tendering process seemed to be becoming superfluous.

They had received a casual letter from an overseas company inquiring about their expertise in a particular area. They sent back a capability statement and a price. Next thing, they received a brief letter telling them the assignment was theirs and asking when they were available to start.

If only business was that easy for everybody. The reality of this situation features is that it was the result of a lot of hard work. This engineering consortium has been active in the Australian market place for more than 50 years. They employ some of the most skilled graduates in the country and they have completed some of the most significant work in Australia.

Nevertheless, there have been times when they may well have fallen into a number of traps. Avoiding these pitfalls is what characterizes a successful firm.

It is clear, that they did not allow their areas of expertise to be determined only by their past experiences. They went to the marketplace and determined what the demand would be in certain areas in the future and developed skills accordingly.

They diversified from one particular industry area into other industry areas to offset the impact of a downturn in one of the market segments in which they were active.

Before it became fashionable, they multi-skilled their professionals to allow a much more versatile staffing of major projects. Also, they converted to the use of contract labor to better manage the supply/demand equation long before others.

All of the above strategies amount to good management of an enterprise and good management of a skill base that constitutes the service that the company provides. The bottom line is that having a great product is no use to you if no-one wants it. As one of my long term colleagues says it's no good selling red tins, when everyone wants blue tins.

Enthusiasm wins

Some years ago, I featured an independent jewelry store that had just turned itself from a modest success into a roaring success by changing location in the same shopping centre. The trick was to be available to the people coming out of the variety store, not the supermarket.

Well I went into this business with a watch repair recently and was delighted to find that the business was better than ever. Spending time chatting to the owner make it easy to see why he just keeps on keeping on. He is a ball of energy.

In addition to having a people personality, this business owner is always getting involved with the community. He sponsors sports teams, enters business achievement awards and doing anything that keeps an edge on the business so that the customer is always getting a 'fresh' approach from the owner and the staff.

This type of approach is very commonly used by some of the most successful cafe and restaurant proprietors. They get involved with their customers. This can be just a chat with a once only customer through to becoming good friends with regulars.

It is interesting to see these successful people have such a great memory for customers' identities in terms of their hobbies, their family and their special tastes in jewelry or food. I believe there is a definite relationship between the positivity that is consistent with this enthusiasm and the ability to remember so much detail and link it to the right customer.

However it works, that enthusiastic and positive approach seems to bring the results, particularly in retail businesses. So use to advantage and make sure you employ people with the same style, you will not be sorry.

Establish common values

So often people ask me 'How do I communicate with my people and get them to work with me as a team?'. The answer is simple - establish common values.

Sit down with your people (all of them if possible, group by group or with representatives) and discuss with them what attitudes and behavior that they and you should share to make the business run well for all concerned. When you have agreed on the values, write them down, publish them and live by them.

That could be the end of this article, but it would only be half of the story. Living by the values will be difficult for you and for the team, because we are all idealists at heart and what we think we do is not necessarily what we really do.

To make the Values Strategy work you have to have simple values that mean something in a day to day business environment, like 'work deadlines will be <u>agreed,</u> by the parties involved' (a value to combat the 'everything is urgent' syndrome).

Also, you have to make sure the values apply universally, not just where it suits you. The word team means share all the time. If the one law for the rich and another for the poor philosophy is part of your make up, you shouldn't start the process.

Clearly, honest implementation is critical to the process and takes some work. If you are genuine (and not just trying to manipulate people), establishing shared values can make a major contribution to your culture and your results.

Find honest suppliers

These days, the suppliers to your business are an integral part of your business success. Indeed, they always have been, but only now is it well and truly recognized how important your supplier is in the health and success of your business.

Domestically, I had the opportunity to see just how different suppliers could be when I took my brush cutter to be repaired.

I thought the first supplier to whom I took the brush cutter was honest and well priced. I had taken my lawn mower there previously and had been quite happy with the service provided.

This supplier had a mechanic who told me that the brush cutter was not worth repairing as the engine was completely worn out. He even showed me the piston and signs of wear indicating that it was no longer in a useable condition.

My first concerns that all might not be well in this situation, arose when a salesman from the dealership immediately tried to sell me a new piece of equipment.

I decided that I would wait and consider my options.

A friend then suggested that if I took the piece of equipment to an authorized dealer, I would at least be able to check that it was beyond repair and I might even be able to get some value as a trade in. So I decided to take this particular action.

Can you imagine my total disbelief and disgust when the dealer advised me that the piece of equipment merely needed tuning up at a cost of $10.00.

I can only hope that this is an isolated incident, because I cannot believe that a genuine error had occurred with the other supplier.

The example I have given certainly reinforced for me the need to be eternally vigilant in relation to any type of supplier and reinforced my belief in trying to develop sound relationships with honest, reliable and competent suppliers.

Certainly, the new supplier I have discovered will be getting all of my business in lawn mowing and related repair areas.

More broadly, I think this little incident reinforces the inevitable inconsistencies in everything in life which includes peoples' capacity to perform consistently to an agreed standard.

Franchise is no panacea

It is sad to be interviewing and counseling a number of competent and previously successful business people, who have had their fingers burned up to the elbows in the franchise market.

As one gentleman told me recently, 'I thought I had prepared extremely well. I had the materials checked carefully by a solicitor and I also thought I knew a fair bit about business.

It turned out that the person selling me the franchise bore an incredible similarity in every way to Arthur Daley of Minder fame.

Nothing that he told me was true, but I believe he honestly had convinced himself that what he said was true'. If you are not familiar with this British television series, any film or television series featuring confidence tricksters will do.

So what can one do to warn people who are getting sucked into these situations and sometimes losing their life savings. The difficulty of instituting preventive measures cannot be overestimated.

One person I spoke to had been on a career transition program with professionally counselors. Unfortunately, the counselors did not even give the basic warning that I use regularly.

My standard comment about self employment is - 'if you were not considering going into business prior to being retrenched then do not think of going into one now', unless there has been some fundamental change in your view about 'working for the man'.

As the person I was speaking to told me, it became clear later that lack of an income and self-esteem issues overshadowed the good sense that was originally available to say 'stop, do not buy yourself a job, invest your money wisely and keep looking for work'.

A sound overall personal investment strategy needs to be put into writing in these circumstances as a constantly visible warning against instituting possibly dangerous and ill thought out strategies. If any such move is contemplated, then advice should be sought from an investment adviser who can give a balanced view about getting a return on funds.

Professionally qualified people in the legal or accounting areas are appropriate to give comments about the technical aspects of the areas covered by their expertise, but cannot give a balanced view about return on funds from a number of comparative investments.

In the final analysis, if you are receiving advice from anyone on how to spend your money and they do not stand to lose anything if you lose, that is about what their advice will be worth. You need someone who will be tied in with you on a long term basis and who will have a very strong vested interest in your future.

You also need to scrutinize, very carefully, the background of any particular individual and totally satisfy yourself that it qualifies them to take on the very important role of having an impact on your future security and the security of your family.

Also, sayings like 'never give a sucker an even break', 'there is a fool born every minute' and 'you can fool some of the people all of the time and all of the people some of the time' apply to you and to me and your next door neighbor not just someone featured in the local newspaper.

Friendliness - it's a product

We see so much effort put into creating tourism products to attract the increasingly discerning visitor and the focus is almost invariably on something you can see or touch.

Perhaps the greatest product of all time has always been right here under our noses, but the packaging of it requires a lot of skill.

I was passing a huddle in the city recently and could not resist peeking into the centre of attention. Two telephone technicians had their street directory out and were playing tour guide to an enthralled group of grey power tourists.

To me this is what the travelling experience is all about. Meeting and talking at some length with the ordinary person who is the real face of the destination. If you talk to people about their best experiences while travelling, you will see this people factor coming through again and again.

One of my golfing buddies tells me he was another Aussie tourist who could only handle 20 churches and 50 sculptures before he started turning his attention to investigating what the locals thought of their home grown product. In other words, did they go visiting churches and looking at sculptures on weekends? If they did not, where did they go? This is where my golfing buddy headed and as part of his aim to have a non-tourist travel experience. He always had some fascinating stories to tell of where he ended up on these many adventures off the beaten track.

The friendly Aussie is legendary, but I get the feeling that there is still room for the legendary Friendly Aussie City. We certainly have the people, along with the weather and the atmosphere, but how do you package the tourist experience that lets you see the people and not just the town that they built? It's a tough one.

Give them money

In speaking with the director of a small business recently, the area of greatest concern was the best way to reward long standing, loyal employees.

The company had a positive performance appraisal system and paid better than average salaries, so the directors were trying to think of more inventive ways to thank their employees over and above their wages.

Holidays, gifts and various other non-cash benefits had been considered but the directors were not sure what the best option would be or whether to give everyone the same benefit.

I think I surprised these company owners when I said quite promptly 'Give them money'. If you want to show your people that you appreciate what they have achieved, use what they have achieved for you.

To me, reward is maximized if the individual is in control of how the benefit is enjoyed.

Certainly, in special circumstances like retirement non-cash gifts of sentimental significance are the way to go (plus money). In general, however, nothing beats the value of cash for rewarding a contribution to the company's profit.

If you are in any doubt, just ask the individual to choose between goods or cash. Provided the choice is genuine, cash will win every time. I was pleased the company, a long term client, decided to reward every employee with and allocated quite a significant sum which was distributed according to a formula I devised that rewarded each employee according to their input over the previous year.[1]

---

[1] The Chairman still provided every employee with a large Christmas ham as he did not want to break a long standing tradition.

Global Performance Indicators (GPIs)

More and more businesses are looking to focus their attention on one particular measure that indicates how successful the business will be.

In other words, instead of waiting till they have finished their financial year and checking on their results, they are looking to find an ongoing indicator that will predict that they are on line to achieve or exceed their financial targets.

One of the very good things about this trend has been its application in not for profit areas. As a result, these public service oriented organizations have been able to measure their performance on an ongoing basis. One of the major challenges is to find a realistic measure and then face up to the fact that most people's performance is not very good.

The level of violent crime is a sound global indicator of government performance. By and large, government is charged with the responsibility of managing a society that is physically and mentally safe for its customers - the public.

In the transport area, both private and public organizations are charged with transporting individuals and goods from point A to point B safely and on time. In fact, the quality, quantity and safety rules are very powerful in terms of creating any performance indicator.

One very well known international firm has based its whole performance assessment system on providing the right product (quality) in full and on time (quantity), and has achieved outstanding results.

At the other end of the scale, the non-violent crime performance indicator for government is all about safety, but is still very powerful.

The key strategy for business is to examine their product or service and determine a GPI. On a trial basis, the GPI should be checked against other retrospective measures of performance.

When the GPI has been validated to be a true predictor of success, it can be used as an ongoing measure of the organizations or individual's performance related activities.

One of the major benefits of having ongoing performance indicators is the immediacy of the reward to individuals within the organization who, more often than not, have felt
quite removed from any results the organization achieves. For this reason, the GPI is often reinforced with numerous other indicators for smaller working groups and finally individual performance indicators, which link back through the system to the GPI.

The most important thing of all is to not be put off by the jargon (like GPI) and realize that the development of these measures can lead to outstanding performance.

So get yourself a GPI, live by it and be one of the modern managers, who looks ahead with certainty instead of looking back in disbelief.

Performance Indicators - Global, Key, whatever.

_____
_____
_____
_____
_____
_____
_____
_____
_____

Images of evil?

One of the areas that appear to have caused greatest stress over many years for hardworking, intelligent and ethical business people is the apparent success of less capable, less hardworking and less ethical competitors or colleagues.

I often counsel people at the mature or closing stages of their career in relation to their personal frustrations at seeing greater reward go to people with a combination of less ability and fewer ethics.

I was fascinated recently to have a discussion with a young person in relation to career choice. As this young woman had already shown quite some practical commercial orientation, I suggested that a career in business might be high on her list of priorities. Her reply was 'if it means ending up like (a certain prominent businessman), I will give it a miss thanks'.

Apparently this quite competent and reasonably ambitious young woman had witnessed a particular businessman's treatment of a person who was neither capable nor appropriately positioned to defend herself. It made a very strong impression on her and certainly took the shine off a business career, if the prospect was that she would end up with a similar personality.

Personally, I was delighted to see such perceptiveness in someone so young, although I was disappointed that a whole category of occupations could stand damned through the actions of one man.

Unfortunately, the assessment seemed accurate enough. Several days later I was telephoned by a very committed and competent secretary who had worked for some years for one of my clients, before he accepted a more senior position in another organization. She told me that she had been sacked without notice and without reason by her new boss, who appeared to have all the characteristics already discussed in the earlier case study.

Apparently this individual worked exclusively on the basis of personal like and dislike. The best way to be liked by him was to feed his ego. This was something that this particular secretary did not feel was part of her professional duties. This man clutched at straws to try to find reasons why he was dismissing this long-serving secretary, but it turned out it was merely to replace her with someone with better 'sucking up' skills.

The positive side of this experience is the imminent arrival into the business sector of people who wish to succeed, but not at the expense of human dignity - either their own or someone else's. I hope there are many more of them.

The major negative side of these two case studies is the clear indication that people in business are still using their authority unchecked to make inequitable decisions. This darker side of the private sector may well be sufficient reason for the large amount of resource already being dedicated to producing legislation to ensure fairness in employment situations.

We can only lament that malevolence remains a characteristic of the human personality

What is my philosophy and how does it rate?

_____

_____

_____

_____

_____

_____

_____

_____

_____

Knuckle down

Everybody has jobs they like less than most. For many people it is doing the accounts, one of the most important jobs in any business.

The answer to this type of problem is just as unsavory as the problem itself. You just have to knuckle down and get on with it. You can ease yourself into it and head off the pressure situation that occurs if you do not wait till pressure from elsewhere is the only motivating factor.

First, choose a specific time which you associate with being low on pressure (and which you probably 'waste' on a favorite job or low priority recreation. Second, decide that you will just 'get started' and do the bulk of the work later.

With the first strategy giving you the best chance of actually doing something and the second lulling you into a false sense of security about not really having to suffer too much, you will find that you actually make a start.

Amazingly, when you get into it, any job is never as bad as you imagined. It is amazing how powerful our mind is at exaggeration of the bad as well as the good.

Finally, when you leave the task, make sure you do so in the middle of something that will let you begin again with the minimum of fear.

Something easy or routine is usually best. You will know when this is because you will not want to stop. Do not leave the job when you get bogged down. This will only reinforce your avoidance behavior.

It sounds simple, but a little bit of time and emotion management can get those 'too hard basket' jobs under control.

Look at the performance indicators

Many corporations are making major changes with the specific aim of improving their customer service.

One corporation that had been a supplier of mine for many years made major changes involving massive redundancies. I was told that the strategy was specifically to improve customer service and that my account would be handed to a new manager in a regional centre dedicated to customer service.

The theory was that Customer service would improve because this specialist manager would not be encumbered by day to day management responsibilities of my previous geographically based service provider and would be able to attend to my customer needs much more efficiently.

Certainly, within a month of the change taking place, I was called by my new Customer Service Manager. I was most pleased to hear from him because I wanted to make a major change in the business that specifically involved this service provider.

Another reason I was very interested to see how the situation might be improved, revolved around the incredibly good service I had received from this individual's predecessor who was a geographically based Branch Manager. If I wanted advice or some action from this previous Branch Manager, results were virtually instantaneous with appointments being made within 24 hours. Also, in attending functions at this Branch Manager's office, I found that his other customers received similar service.

You can imagine my reaction, when my request for an appointment with the new Customer Service Manager resulted in a promise of a call back sometime in the next fortnight. Even worse, the new Customer Service Manager's reply was full of comments about <u>his</u> needs - his need to take recreation leave, his need to fit me into his busy schedule and his need to have the time to study my file.

Of all the excuses, the time to study my file may have been valid, but in my view it should have been studied before I was called, especially since in the type of business that he was in, it was very likely that I was going to ask very specific questions.

In my view, this organization has not done its homework. The only way it will detect quickly that its strategy is an incorrect one will be to assess performance indicators. One of its major performance indicators should be that customers receive the right advice in a timely fashion.

There are only two factors in question here, correctness and timeliness, and having struck out on one already, they cannot hope to score more than fifty percent.

So if you are looking at making some major changes, try to research carefully what the outcomes will be. If you cannot know exactly what the outcomes will be, monitor what they are very quickly in the short term.

You may discover that what seems an amazingly efficient move on your part is not very effective when your various customers become disaffected and leave you in droves. In this area, an ounce of prevention is definitely worth many pounds of cure.

How do you measure your customer service levels?

_____
_____
_____
_____
_____
_____
_____
_____
_____
_____
_____
_____

Looking good

Good times and bad times come and go in business and you strive on. Your customers, however, prefer to think that everything is going well all the time. Nobody likes to think that a business is in any sort of trouble. So why do some businesses advertise that they might be doing poorly?

A sign on a local retail outlet says in meter high fluorescent lettering 'Back to School Specials'. School has been back for months (it probably feels like years to the students and teachers). Other signs on the shop front are older (much older) and look it. What does this mean?

It probably means that the shop is so busy that the owner has just not had time to think about signage, but the opposite is the image presented. Hopefully, the impact on the business will be minimal, but it might not be.

Tired! That is the word used to describe businesses or ideas that have had their day. It is not nice and it can be reversed so easily, but the damage is often done before the owners or managers realize and then getting it right can be a real problem.

I recall the head architect at a large corporation where I worked many years ago explaining to me the strategy of his daily inspection of the 100 hectare site on which the corporation's head office was situated.

'Quality in presentation is no accident', he said. 'It has be planned in the greatest detail and policed vigilantly. Even the slightest slip is noticeable, even if it is sub-consciously. The job of inspection is a specific one that has to be given specific time and a specific routine.'

You may not be able to afford your own architect, but you must afford the time and a plan to keep your business looking good. This includes all aspects of every business. Shop front, interior, displays, stationery and on it goes. You must be able to say with confidence - looking good, feeling good, doing well!

Loyalty - a thing of the past?

In speaking to a group of representatives from some of Australia's largest manufacturing companies, the conversation turned to the issue of customer loyalty.

These representatives were unanimous in their view that customer loyalty was essentially a thing of the past. Probably one of the saddest parts of the conversation was hearing that the tremendous amount of effort and other resources put into producing the ultimate in customer service had made the representatives feel as though they had boxed themselves into a corner.

Apparently, now the customers expected the ultimate in customer service from every point of view, but still felt they had the right to use information from the various suppliers to get better prices from other suppliers. While friendships and some loyalties established over many years continued, it was clear from speaking to these people that doing business was not the pleasurable experience that it had been in the past.

Another interesting aspect to this discussion was the difficulty of gaining acceptance of locally made products. Apparently, one of the largest contracts to come up for installation of one of the company's products had automatically specified an overseas product on quality grounds without the least thought that a local company could meet the order. Fierce intervention by the company's Chief Executive opened the door for this local manufacturer, but the ignorance and I would say a large element of 'cultural cringe' has been clearly displayed by this event.

It seems that this country's largest and highest quality manufacturers are not always respected by the best designers, who think it enhances their profile to specify international products. Unfortunately, they do not see Australian products as being international. This is cultural cringe with a devastating economic impact.

So nationally, there seems to be an anti-loyalty movement. The theme of 'a prophet is never recognized at home' is alive and well to the detriment of all of us.

The smart business person will realize the opportunity in this area and build a business network based on loyalty and awareness of their high quality local products and their commitment to local productivity. Particularly, they will promote this commitment to their shareholders, owners, and employees. The result will benefit everyone in the community.

MBWA - alive, well and still effective

A senior manager in an organization consulted me recently on problems he felt were occurring because people at the coalface really did not have sufficient access to him.

He attributed the access problem to particular supervisors and he was working on that problem but things were going just too slowly. He wanted my advice on how to get a quick fix to alleviate the problems associated with the lack of immediate access by supervisors to him.

'Management by walking around', I said: 'It may be old, but it is still very effective'.

Naturally, he knew about management by walking around (MBWA), having learned about it in theory and practiced it on previous occasions. On this occasion however, he was just so close to the problem, that the very basics were not obvious to him.

So we had a lengthy discussion and revised the principles of MBWA. I told him not to hesitate to get out there and have the closest possible look at what everybody is doing. Make sure that you approach this activity in a very supportive way. Do not be seen as the inspector or ogre from head office who is there to check on everybody.

Make it very clear that you are there to lend any support necessary to make sure the job is well done, but you still want to know in absolute detail what is going on, how the job is being done and exactly who is doing what.

I was delighted when I received a call from the same manager some weeks later to tell me that MBWA was alive, well and still very effective. His management by walking around had an instant effect and totally brought the problem under control.

So if you feel that you are not getting access to information you need in the management role you occupy, or in any job you do for that matter, or if you feel that people are not getting access to you when they should be, just do some MBWA. It is very simple and very effective, but sometimes you just can't see the obvious solutions because they are so simple.

Management by walking around is like exercise, you have to do it on a regular basis to keep yourself totally trim and to keep your organization's activities trim as well. Get used to doing it regularly, you will find it refreshing for you and for the people who work with you.

MBWA - When did you last do it?
How can you fit it into your schedule?

Mentoring - simple and effective

A high school work experience student came in to our office for a week to find out what a psychologist does on a day to day basis. Although her time in our office was most productive in a general way, I discovered that her real interest was in a specialized area of psychology which was only available through a certain part of the public sector.

I followed formal channels to attempt to obtain an appointment for this young lady with an appropriate person in the organization that she was wishing to eventually join. After three telephone calls with different people and a potential referral to a fourth, I gave up on that particular line of approach.

Fortunately, I was acquainted with one of the very senior operatives in the same area and, not wanting to be told by yet another person in Human Resources that they were too busy and it was just too difficult, I asked him for assistance. Without hesitation, he arranged for the work experience student to spend an hour with exactly the person whose job she would like to be in, in ten years time.

The whole exercise took considerably less trouble than the excuses provided by the three human resource professionals, who went to great pains to explain to me how difficult the whole exercise would be and to really not bother to pursue the next person in the chain.

The tragedy in this whole exercise is that the people who should understand most about the motivating process in work and society were the ones who contributed most to de-motivating this particular student.

Mentoring is essentially a process where individuals provide guidance, usually in an informal way, to others who are wishing to develop in areas of skill possessed by the mentor. This one hour session, although relatively short (mentoring can go on for years), is an example of mentoring in action.

In many cases, the mentoring process is an informal one between parent and child, senior student and junior student and so on. It also can be very formal as with academic study program and professional supervision.

The most important aspect of mentoring is the willingness of the mentor to provide information and guidance to the student in an open and motivating style to encourage the student to develop their abilities to the maximum possible level.

Clearly, my staff and I adopted a short term mentoring role with our work experience student. In fact, I was delighted with the positive critique given by this young woman on one of my own programs on job hunting because it highlighted the capacity of people at all levels to contribute to the development and implementation of work ideas.

Mentoring can be an extremely positive process for both the mentor and the student. It only requires a positive outlook, a constructive well planned approach and a basic understanding of the principles of learning.

Oh, the hypocrisy of it

A government purchasing group conducted a public session recently to educate potential suppliers in relation to their requirements.

One of their major requirements for products and services was substantial Australian content. The representative of my organization who was in attendance was optimistic, but skeptical, knowing how these words often ring very hollow in execution. Nevertheless, he was determined to keep an open mind.

Can you believe that upon being given a purchasing information folder for a particular department and lifting the flap to read the contents, the first words that he read under the flap were: 'Made in England'.

What can one say? What can one do? When the tunes that large government enterprises sing for their suppliers are not the ones they dance to, credibility is gone. The paper was not even recycled.

We have our own government bleating about how unfair other government corporations are to us as a state or a nation. I wonder if that is where they learn about how to treat their own constituents?

On a positive note, I recall a very senior director from a large company making it very clear that locally made applied as much to the people that they hired as to the products that they bought. In his case, he practiced what he preached, but then he did have total control over the business enterprise.

How do we bring some change to this hypocritical situation which has the double whammy of not only spending the public's money on overseas products, but has the public's representatives telling local voters who want to be suppliers that they must have significant local content to sell to the government?

Unfortunately, the answer is not an easy one. The difficulty of working with governments and supplying to governments is virtually legend. The fact that our system is such that many are allowed to believe that they are the master and we are the servants does little to help the situation. Fortunately, some Chief Executives have very enlightened attitudes and are bringing about significant changes in attitude.

In the final analysis, it must go back to individuals and their representative groups to keep pushing the barrow of the interests of the community. I know that one major supplier is publicly pursuing that strategy at the moment.

Each of us, in whatever way is available to us, must make our thoughts known and encourage the consideration of options which are in the best interests of the community. After all we supply the funds and own the enterprise.

Old ways are hard to eradicate

It was staggering to hear recently of a leading corporation that was undergoing its second restructure within two years and moving away from a very flat management structure to rebuild the pyramid that existed two years before.

Change for the sake of change I thought had disappeared, as had newly appointed senior executives imposing their will on organizations purely to show 'who is the boss'. It certainly seems this is not the case.

One of the most frustrating things for employees is the inability to gain access through to senior people because of the tangled corporate structure. To see people creating this tangled web as a new strategy for success sends a chill up my spine.

Apparently the feeling and talk in this organization already is that people further <u>down</u> in the organization will sink deeper. Having worked for ten years to eliminate the mushroom syndrome (keep them in the dark and feed them on compost), I can only hope that employees now are more personally able to express their disquiet.

Another option is to join the majority and just ride the wave and not swim against the current. The only trouble is that the wave and the boat riding it, only has seats for ten people and there are hundreds in the water.

A bit dramatic perhaps, but one has to dramatize sometimes to get some awareness of just how downtrodden people can become in a hierarchical or pyramid system of management.

As one of my senior consultants is so fond of saying 'There are still people who are using management techniques that were invented in the same year as the pop up toaster'. The real problem is that they are still out there in positions where they can have the same negative impact they had twenty years ago.

Time brings positive changes for some, but for others, retrograde steps are still being taken that lose track of the bigger picture and ignore the benefits of allowing people to take responsibility and develop at all levels.

Hopefully there will not be too many 'throwback managers' who will lead us back to the age of the dinosaurs. However, employees have to be active in developing their skill levels to combat these problems.

Alternatively, with good skills, employees can move to more productive organizations with informed management styles that make good use of the employee's skills.

Personal development for business

A major activity for me over the last few years has been conducting personal development programs for members of large industrial and commercial organizations. This may not sound unusual, but the content of the programs is not what you might expect.

More and more, the focus in business is genuinely turning to the people 'complexion' of the organization so that my programs contain more about managing yourself than managing the work that you do.

The philosophical basis for this shift is that people who are confident about their life, their relationships and their careers are more productive.

The formula works with greater numbers of people adopting a self management role at work, reducing the management bureaucracy, cutting costs and being happier with the opportunity to share in the benefits.

There is a double whammy in the process, because the development training results in the management upward phenomenon that so many people talk about, but can only show you in theory. Practical examples of self management plus upward management of the management team speak for themselves.

Once the practice of self management is achieved, significant financial benefits are quickly evident. If they are not, then you are on the wrong track.

It is a little elusive, because the understanding of true self confidence at work is something of an art, but there is no better time to start the process. The structural changes in the workplace mean the successful groups will be those which trust, communicate and grow together.

Personality has impact

I conducted a minor transaction at one of the largest banks in the country and, contrary to all my usual experiences, was assisted by an individual who injected her personality into the exchange naturally but with a great amount of impact.

As I said to her 'Has the bank finally included some customer service training in its training and development program? This would have to be the most genuinely friendly service I have ever experienced at any branch of this bank'?

After a little further discussion, it became clear that this good service was not the result of training but of selection. This particular operative possessed a bright and cheery personality and was able to develop rapport with customers in a natural and very effective way.

Within days of the above incident, two of Australia's largest corporations released their results and both Chief Executives stated that they believed their return to sound levels of profitability was directly related to a greater emphasis on selecting the right people to provide customer service.

When it is considered that both these organizations employ tens of thousands of people, this is not an easy task. In both cases, it had taken years to rectify a stultified and stuffy corporate culture and produce one that was totally focused towards the needs, both emotional and physical, of the customer.

I hasten to add that if these people rest on their laurels and do not adopt an attitude of continuous improvement, they will soon be back where they started.

The importance of customer service is spoken about often these days, but it really needs a demonstration of its wide ranging impact on profitability to be taken seriously.

The customer service model of

> Personality to establish rapport with the customer,
> Investigation of the customer's needs,
> Inspiration to establish the confidence of the customer,
> Closing the transaction successfully, and
> Service as a key part of the reason for being in business

all need to be preached, practiced and perfected.

Selecting staff who have the ability and personality to reach the required standard is essential. It is amazing how many firms still do not have any formal selection process. This means that they fail to satisfy equity requirements and do themselves a great disservice in not selecting the best person for the job.

Only with a sound selection process based on a job description and person specification can effective selection take place. It certainly requires effort, but the benefits are enormous.

Pride and Discipline

Watching lifesavers stand by while two drunken youths threw a half full bottle of drink backwards and forwards in the flagged area, with children nearby, made me realize again just how easy it is to slip up in our approach to our work duties.

Assuming they had authority and responsibility, I asked the three guards on duty if they were going to do something about it or whether I should.   Their hesitation was even more concerning. Finally, they took action and it was not a drama.

If you take on a job, paid or voluntary, do it properly. If you do not know the limit of your authority and responsibility - ask!

The flow on of poor performance is a danger that all organizations need to guard against. You may work hard to establish a good standard, but you have to work twice as hard to maintain it. So how do you?

The basic principles of instruction require that you realize that you have to change attitudes as well as convey information in a training setting.

If you are training someone in a policing role, for example, they have to know the exact limits of their power, but they also have to understand the social background to their role and have a sense of pride and discipline in how they do the job.

Other areas are no different! Handling complaints, cleaning a car, delivering a message - all activities can have challenges that test your sense of pride in your job and your discipline in performing it.

In the final analysis however, the basic issue is - if you are going to do anything, do it properly.

Profit without injury

It was most refreshing to have a lengthy conversation recently with a high flying manager from one of our most successful organizations.

He happened to raise an issue which is one of my hobby horses - the questioning of Total Quality Management (TQM) and other acronyms.

This executive put forward very strongly a convincing argument for the successful management of companies without the frills associated with the latest management theories.

What impressed me most was this very hard driving and very profit-oriented executive's strong belief that the absolute personal safety of workers was the most critical factor for an organization's success.

He was adamant that there was never, never, never any excuse for personal injury to workers because safe working practices were an integral part of efficient working practices.

In pursuing his argument, he was most fired up about the fact that TQM and other gimmicks (as he described them) provided a cop-out option for managers who lacked the general management skill to bring together the right team to combine effective marketing with operational efficiency and deliver a profit to the shareholders.

I was inspired by this rare moment of expansiveness from this individual. I knew from experience within the organizations that he had worked with that he was highly regarded as a tough but fair straight shooting operator.

It had been explained to me how he had acquired a reputation for increasing the personal net worth of both shareholders and employees without a major fuss.

Are we looking for 'The promised land' while the farm under our feet sprouts weeds as a result of our neglect and lack of skill? I think there is certainly a strong indication that many managers are having trouble following the basic plan and are happy to follow any new scheme for potential salvation.

Worse still, I believe many of these schemes have been institutionalized and now feed off their own swarm of flies that have gathered around the smell of a good feed.

Till now, the only spanner in the works of the purveyors of the latest management gimmick has been the retrenched workers littering the corporate streets.

Fortunately, there seems to be something of a new order among those rising in more successful companies. This new order has the confidence in its abilities and is not scared to say that success can be achieved simply if one is prepared to take personal responsibility.

In the corporate world, profit is the goal, but people are the soul. Managers who understand and accept this value will succeed in the long term and build a better corporate entity for the community.

Certainly, there have been sufficient examples of how not to do it, and undermining managers' confidence in themselves and their willingness is just one of them.

On the other hand, building of personal value and respect for others as espoused by my high flying companion is a simple an effective strategy that has my support and I would recommend it as a sound business strategy.

Psychological services must be user friendly

For as long as I have provided psychological assessment services to businesses, I have insisted that the results obtained by individuals should be verbally 'fed back' to them and discussed as an integral part of the assessment process.

I have always felt that to do psychological assessments and not provide the individual with the results and not incorporate their comments where appropriate in the resulting report, is clearly omitting one important aspect of the process.

For this reason, it was very disappointing to hear again recently of incidents where testing was being conducted without individuals being able to gain access to the results. In addition to failing to get the full picture, the process alienated and agitated senior business people from the psychological assessment service providers and from their client.

In pursuing one of my main development themes of helping people stay in control of matters affecting their livelihood, I constantly tell people that they must not agree to these testing sessions or even less formal assessment measures before ensuring that they will be told their results and be able to discuss them with a professional qualified to conduct the assessments.

Legislation in this area is weak, leaving individuals very much at the mercy of the marketplace. In this way, the person being assessed is left rely on their own self confidence and negotiation skills to share in the results of the assessment and people are often caught out on the day and do not get achieve this goal.

Finding themselves in unfamiliar circumstances, people are very unlikely to be demanding. When an assessment is taking place, people need to concentrate much more on the challenges at hand rather than thinking about negotiating their position on the day. This artificially created relationship of superior and subordinate has to be managed in the most professional way possible.

Also, "psychological" services which are not called by that name can be provided by a wide range of people who are in the business of assessing others. In certain cases, material can be obtained from an organization by a qualified individual and then left behind for use by other non-qualified members of the organization.

This can be quite dangerous and businesses need to be aware that lack of skill in dealing with matters which impact so directly on people's self-esteem, can do significant damage to their corporate image with possible attendant losses in customer loyalty, supplier trust and employee commitment.

All people like to control the things that are important in their lives. Their view about themselves is very important and go right to the heart of their existence. To forget this can be one of businesses hardest lessons.

How much do you know about what is important to the people who are important to you?

_____
_____
_____
_____
_____
_____
_____
_____
_____
_____
_____
_____
_____
_____
_____
_____
_____
_____
_____
_____
_____
_____
_____
_____
_____

Psychology- still a luxury?

In reading a document recently about the interests and profiles of public company directors, it was disappointing to see reinforced the general philosophy that accounting, law and operations were the prime areas of experience for directors and the main areas of interest pursued by directors.

It should not surprise you then that in a counseling session with a student who had deferred law studies for 12 months with thoughts of pursuing a career in psychology, I was able to confidently say that the psychology/human resources area within business enterprise remains a luxury area.

Interestingly, no-one up to the time of our discussion had been able to indicate clearly to this law student why study of the law and a law degree was a good thing from a business point of view.

Anyone spoken to had merely shrugged their shoulders and said 'Well, you know, it's a good thing'.

A basic examination of the establishment, conduct and winding up of any activity in life gives a clear clue as to the reasons why law is a good thing from a career point of view.

Perhaps it is more of a good thing than it should be, however, because of our inability to get past the basics.

If you examine the commitment and enthusiasm amongst senior people for the people side of their enterprise, it is often fairly shallow. For many years professionals and company executives in the areas of human resources and related fields have spoken about preaching to the converted and doing business with themselves.

The people business can get a lot of attention, but how often does it really get a first place in the discussion of how the business is going and how the business can be improved.

Once again, in speaking to a senior human resource professional from one of Australia's largest companies, it was clear that he was not happy with the company strategy of cutting back heavily on human resource activities in all areas. He felt that, at a time when hundreds of people were being retrenched and numerous jobs were being relocated to others states, human resource expertise was needed more than ever.

In government circles as well, the focus is supposed to be on human skill development and empowerment as the way of the future, but development of bureaucratic systems is more and more oriented towards distrust.

Generally, a multiplicity of systems to reduce individual decision making and responsibility seems to be preferred to development of overall management skills which are measured on effectiveness.

The business that perfects the psychology of the enterprise and relates it to its effectiveness will easily outstrip its competitors.

Regrettably, achieving this goal is much more difficult than it sounds and many organizations give up long before they get anywhere near understanding the goal, let alone achieving it.

Quality Assurance be damned, price is the key

The response to my criticisms of quality management has been most interesting.

A senior executive, who recently retired from a very large organization rang to tell me how he had been making similar comments to his organization for years as it progressively suffered from reducing revenue and reducing profit while introducing every conceivable form of external quality system.

In his view, the company and its executives had lost the plot and were not prepared or able to take responsibility for the performance of the organization. They use these external systems as crutches, he said, and they were most unsuccessful in their attempt to prevent further decline in the performance of the organization.

Closer to home, an academic colleague of mine sent me some literature and gave me the example of a local firm that had invested quite some money in taking out externally certified quality assurance, but discovered that it didn't matter who had quality assurance in supplying for the government, the lowest price still won the tender.

Further, it was mentioned to me that a company that set up a fictitious organization it organized to have quality assured. This organization put in spectacularly low bids and also won the business, before revealing that it did not exist.

My academic friend is scathing about industries needing to waste spectacular amounts of money on having other people tick the box to indicate that they are able to produce a product at a level that is satisfactory for the consumer.

A scam, a racket, a fad or just a large group of well intention people trying to help industry - what is quality management?

As one of my clients liked to say, the staff of the State Bank of Victoria were incredibly well intention and worked incredibly hard and managed to squander $2.4 billion.

The quality management area has a lot of the characteristics of the State Bank of Victoria. A lot of process, a lot of ballyhoo, a lot of money changing hands and a lot of feeling very good in a huge fog that normally occurs when hot air meets cold hard cash.

The bottom line is that there are numerous companies around whose products are essential to the community but do not have quality assurance. No-one is shutting them down. Similarly, the lowest price is still winning the bid and no-one is asking those companies if they have quality assurance.

Companies are still getting into trouble even though they have quality assurance, but nobody is talking about that.

All in all, quality management and many things associated with it have the characteristic that my senior executive was so pleased to point out - people not wanting to take responsibility for general management of their organization. They opt out and go for third party endorsement rather than going with the old saying that 'the buck stops here'.

Looking more broadly, the buck stops all over the place, and it has to because so many companies are just not doing any good no matter what sort of external certification they have.

If you want to succeed in business take personal responsibility for how your company performs and produce a product that people want and will buy from you because it is a good product not because someone else tells them that you are a good manufacturer with a seal of approval. In the final analysis, commerce and industry is about a free market. Quality management in all its forms is just another government impost that reduces the bottom line and keeps money away from shareholders and from employees.

Fortunately, there seems to be a strong ground swell of senior managers and business proprietors who agree with this proposition and it may well be as my academic friend indicated, "Merely a fad that will last several more years and then disappear leaving nothing in its wake of any value".

Forget other peoples' definitions. What does quality mean to you?

Quality is not complicated

Currently, there is a lot of intense discussion about the difficulty and expense of obtaining quality certification. Quality managers are being appointed on all sides, consultants abound and there is a flurry of activity where none existed before.

Despite all this intense activity and good intent, many companies still fail to achieve the certification which they are seeking. It has been suggested to me that in many cases it is because a mountain has been made out of a molehill.

A senior Operations Manager who has installed quality systems on a variety of sites and has achieved certification first time, every time believes that the KIS Principal is still the way to go.

This particular manager Keeps It Simple and consistently hits the jackpot. On one occasion, he tells me, the system was so simple that he was not sure that it even warranted certification. However, because it was a documented true representation of the circumstances and met the requirements, he went ahead.

Sure enough despite, and perhaps because of, almost painful simplicity certification was forthcoming.

Interestingly, a colleague of this individual in the accounting area was able to put forward similar experiences at general management level. He had worked as a troubleshooter in a variety of companies and found that invariably they had come to grief by straying from the Keep It Simple message. Well dressed senior executives with voluminous reports had led these companies to implement strategies which were spectacularly unsuccessful.

In his view, just a basic dose of common sense could have saved these companies, but they pursued relentlessly the 'bells and whistles' strategies that had been supplied to them by their elegantly tailored senior executives.

So, after laboring the point to hammer home the Keep It Simple message, I hope it is clear that quality assurance certification or the quality of general management strategies are decided not by the weight of the materials, but by their content.

Basically, if you cannot understand it, you cannot certify or use it. In other words, an understandable, simple and probably cheap system beats a weighty, complicated and probably very expensive system, every time.

Select carefully, lead honestly

Too many times I have met with people who have rushed into a job which offered big opportunities only to find out that the promised commission never eventuated when the job was won.

Previously, my warnings were directed at the 'would be' overnight success who did not get a written contract or witnesses to a verbal one. Now I feel the evidence is suggesting that the bad deal benefits neither party.

Certainly, some of these unscrupulous employers have moved on leaving a succession of disillusioned and poorer ex-employees behind them. Most that I have tracked, however, have had a relatively brief history due to the poor management which comes out so clearly in their personnel management.

To develop a sound long term business, you should select your new people carefully to ensure the benefits of the contract will give both what they work for and earn. Also, the development process is not guaranteed by the passage of time.

You must lead your people honestly, with as full an awareness of your weaknesses and theirs as you can determine. It is very sad that on the one hand that a manager or owner sees an admission of some weakness as unacceptable.

On the other hand it is worse that so many employees see an admission of some failing by their boss as giving them some greater power rather that an opportunity to be part of a successful team where ones strengths makes up for another's weaknesses.

Employers should select new team members who are aware of what a team is and then treat them with respect and total honesty. Employees should only work with a team that has these characteristics. You will both be winners.

Self discipline must be taught

Excellent I thought, when seeing a representative of a large financial group and property owner cleaning the doors and surrounds of a lift in a city shopping centre.

He was very neatly presented with the emblem of his employer emblazoned on his beautifully tailored work-shirt.

Can this get any better I thought? Next he is going to offer to carry my parcels down to the car park.

As if to teach me a lesson, he turned around and there, perched neatly between his lips, were the remains of a cigarette.

While I watched, he dropped the cigarette on the ground, ground it onto the tiles and kicked the ash and the cigarette butt nonchalantly off to one side.

After the cigarette incident, this wonderful operative immediately returned to polishing the lift doors and inspecting them closely for any speck of dirt. He entered the lift with me and proceeded to polish the inside with great enthusiasm and care.

So what can we learn from this incident and what does it tell us about being more successful in business.

First, it tells us that because a person does one job well, it does not follow that they are aware of the bigger picture. In other words, they may be totally unaware of the negative impact of what they perceive as actions that are unrelated to the performance of their duties.

Second, it shows that clothes do not make the person. Putting a neat uniform on a person and teaching them the right words to say, does not give them in-depth skills in customer service.

These come from an understanding of the organization's mission and the factors that are critical to successful achievement of the organization's goals.

Third, it shows that there remains a place for discipline, self discipline, in every work situation. Also, discipline has to be taught.

I recall many years ago working with a large contract cleaning group, where the cleaning of a toilet was analyzed to determine the safest and fastest method that attained the required standard.

The manager of that organization felt that self discipline in general work behavior and in specific tasks was a training challenge. He made this a key part of both operator and supervisor training.

If you want people to show self discipline, you have to define it, teach it and control it.

She will be back on Wednesday

Even in these very difficult times, it is amazing how the mentality is maintained that business can wait.

I telephoned a high profile and supposedly fast moving commercial real estate group recently to make an inquiry about leasing. I was advised by the receptionist that the individual who dealt with that property was on holidays but I could speak to her secretary.

Upon speaking to the secretary, I explained my requirements and expected to be advised of the details or to be referred to another consultant. Not today!

In response to my detailed explanation about my need for information about particular properties, the secretary replied: "Del will be back on Wednesday" (This was Monday).

I politely but firmly advised her that I did not need the information on Wednesday, I needed it today. The call was promptly interrupted and I found myself speaking to the receptionist again. I was then referred to another consultant.

What is it that results in organization's still not extending the responsibility and authority to team members to ensure that business goes on without 'hiccups'? The answer may lie in a conversation I had on the same day with a human resources specialist attempting to introduce change in a large organization in the industrial sector.

This particular specialist was lamenting the fact that it seemed impossible to get people to think in different ways and hence change the organization to a situation of greater productivity. He was of the view that individuals would rather see the ship go down than give up even one of the advantages they had gained over their fellow employees.

Perhaps survival of the fittest is much more prevalent in our work society than we are aware. It certainly seems to be a factor which makes team building particularly difficult.

Unfortunately, I think the enemy within (managers who preach change, but continue with the old style) is still very real. Whether it is in their own organization or in another, this keeps employees very wary. For this reason, organizations who seek to implement new cooperative systems, need to be completely genuine in word and deed.

On the other hand, I believe long term strategies used by workers to attain security of employment by limiting responsibility have worked very well in the past. It will be hard for many people to abandon these strategies and take risks.

Going beyond the basic brief is the hallmark of a potentially very successful organization. Unfortunately, arriving at this particular meeting of the minds between a receptive workgroup and a suitably enlightened management requires an overcoming of fear on both sides.

I believe our capacity to work with our own feelings in these situations is still limited. Many cultural factors reinforce the limiting of responsibility and the strategy of personal insulation from involvement.

For this reason, I believe that the overcoming of the overall fear of involvement is an essential part of creating good work systems. Within the situation created in the work environment, it is possible to facilitate a cooperative effort to achieve greater productivity, but great skill is needed to bring about the right circumstances for this to occur. Too often, the effort is made but not sustained for anywhere near long enough to get a good result.

As I mentioned to one of my favorite customers in management development, you need to be persistent, insistent and consistent with your message and this can take years.

Communication, Contribution and Accountability - What do you do to encourage it?

_____

_____

_____

_____

_____

_____

_____

_____

_____

_____

_____

_____

_____

_____

_____

_____

Signs of business health

It is interesting that there are so many accounting and legal matters that must be attended to in keeping a business functioning.

Regrettably, these accounting and legal requirements, for the most part, only ensure that the business stays alive (something like a life support system) but do not contribute to the business being fit and productive.

The factors which contribute most to a business' good health are discretionary and often forgotten. The following seven basic characteristics can be used as a mini-audit to determine just how much work has been undertaken in your organization to ensure its good health.

A current strategic plan in writing which is used as a framework for all major business ventures.

- Up-to-date market information in the form of a written marketing plan using the best available market research results.

- A simple and functional document setting out the agreed conditions of work in the enterprise.

- Clear descriptions of the company structure, however flexible, and individual and group authority and responsibilities.

- A formal communication process to allow all employees to share relevant information.

- Documented career paths, training needs and goals for all employees.

- Performance review procedures which involve the employees in open discussion of goal setting and reward distribution.

When one sees a list of this type, the temptation is always to rush in and do them all at once. The normal end result in this circumstance is that a small part of each exercise is completed and no one exercise is completed perfectly. My view is that any one of these exercises undertaken completely is better than undertaking a small part of several of the exercises.

Most importantly, have a careful look at your organization and see where, in any of these areas, you might improve and make your organization more healthy and productive. Fix that one properly and then do the others in turn.

Sneaky techniques do not pay

In speaking with the receptionist of a small branch of a large international organization recently, I was fascinated to find that she had been instructed never to give out the name of her manager to people that telephoned.

Apparently, this person would only speak to people who knew him personally and all other calls were to be directed to the office manager.

Happily, I spoke to the office manager about my particular inquiry and was entirely satisfied with the outcome.

I could not resist asking, however (I can be a real nuisance sometimes when on the scent of a story), both the receptionist and the office manager, why this person was so adamant about protecting his identity from casual inquiries.

Apparently, the heart of the problem lay in the regular calls that all managers receive (me included) from people who say that they know you personally even though you have never met them.

It amazes me that salespeople do not realize, by thinking of their own experience in similar cases, that this type of behavior is really so counterproductive.

It gives them a bad image, it gives their company a bad image and it gives their product or service a bad image. They are not going to be a success in their sales career by trickery.

Certainly, desperate times have been thought by many people to require desperate measures.

Actions of this type bred from desperation, however, will only result in the situation becoming more desperate, not only for the individual but for everyone associated with the company.

It has always been my view that a positively and confidently presented statement about the benefits and competitive advantages of the particular product or service is the best way to succeed in a selling situation.

With regard to accessing the decision maker, I have always operated on the principle that if a decision maker has executive staff at any level who are assigned the responsibility of dealing with inquiries, these people should be recognized.

More success comes from working with these people and according them the respect they deserve for the responsibilities they have, than trying to trick them and cut them out of the picture.

Using one's skill to establish rapport with the receptionist, secretary, purchasing officer or other appropriate person is as much part of the selling process as the written presentation or personal presentation to the decision maker.

So while I think our anonymous state manager has adopted something of an unusual technique, I believe there is merit in all salespeople considering the reasons behind it and using their improved understanding of the negative impact of trickery and making sure they never resort to these techniques.

So few good managers

It is sad that the following anecdote is so common in my experience.

Recently, I was speaking to a senior employee who was very disappointed that a good manager, whom she had been working for, had left the organization.

In expressing her concern about the likely ability of a replacement, she told me that the manager, who had recently resigned, was only the second manager of any ability that she had experienced in a 25 year working career. Is it possible that Australia has so few good managers?

Having personal knowledge of the manager who had most recently supervised this individual, I was aware that she had certainly been supervised by one of the better managers that I have encountered.

Nevertheless, the story sounded just all too familiar to be dismissed as a freak incident.

When I gave the matter more thought, I felt this person was right. There are very few really high quality managers and there seems to be a number of basic reasons why.

First, management requires a definite set of personality characteristics for successful performance as a leader, but these are often not defined well in the Position Description.

Second, there are a set of defined organizational skills that must be acquired to perform successfully in a management role, but the description of these often bears no resemblance to reality.

Third, acquiring the leadership and management skills necessary to be successful as a manager is a lot more demanding that most people acknowledge, so little appropriate effort is invested.

Unfortunately, with respect to the leadership component, many people feel they have this set of characteristics from birth and can cope with any situation. Usually, most people who they supervise in the future do not agree with this view, but the individual never finds out.

With respect to the management skills component, a similar situation arises. Many managers never develop the awareness that their management skills are lacking, let alone that they lack the ability to create, administer and enforce an appropriate set of operational guidelines for a group of people.

So, with many people remaining ignorant of the actual demands of the position of manager, it is unlikely that we are in for any improvements. Overall, our standards are just too low and too poorly defined for this situation to improve in the short term. This is evidenced by repeated episodes of incompetence at the most senior levels.

I know these sweeping generalizations suggest disaster, but quite frankly, I believe we need to be much more self critical if we are to succeed in business at a global level.

Something from nothing

So often I am asked the best strategy for starting a successful business. These days my standard answer is 'Look around you and see what catches your eye'.

At the School of Arts Cafe in Queanbeyan, New South Wales, anyone can see what catches their eye and witness the creation and maintenance of a successful business from no more than the ingenuity and the dedication of the proprietors.

The site is modest. The location is unspectacular. The idea when first mooted must have seemed very ambitious, and perhaps a little crazy. The end result is spectacular.

The internal fit-out is simple, but the walls are adorned with framed tributes to the artists who have appeared there over the years. Sounds simple, but this country theatre cafe/restaurant reminded me of the Carnegie Deli in New York where the walls are similarly decorated with photos of internationally famous patrons.

I do not make lightly the comparison of this local attraction to one of the best known venues in the world. In its own way the School Of Arts Cafe is world class, because it is classy.

These days too many new businesses are established with all the trappings that are supposed to give a classy image which allows the new owner to charge classy prices.

Unfortunately, too often the two do not match and the customer is left wondering what the fuss and high prices are all about.

More disappointingly, the failure of many businesses is contributing to losses for hardworking people and a generally unhealthy small business economy.

One of the answers is to trust your own initiative and invest in your own ideas, rather than using tired formulas that may make you feel secure, but are no substitute for classic originality.

Above all, something new is your own property and means that you are building an asset that is definable and firmly attached to you as the creator. Your commitment is rewarded both extrinsically as well as intrinsically.

Structure for success

It has been very 'in' for people to talk about flattening the organization's structure for some years now.

Watching management strategies like this become trendy is very enjoyable and we can only hope that the effectiveness of organizations will be improved through appropriate restructuring of their management systems.

It is very common to find organizations where numerous levels of management have developed even in relatively small groups.

I recall analyzing a small division of a large public company. This division had only about 40 employees but had developed 11 reporting levels, from the individuals who are involved in day to day work activities (and there weren't too many of them) up to the level where the Chief Executive reported to the Board of Directors.

Market pressures resulted in this part of the organization disappearing with employees being reassigned to other areas, but the way it was allowed to stumble on before this happened is very instructive.

To enhance or preserve jobs, management for many years has created supervisory roles.

Unfortunately, many of these supervisory roles were supervisory in name only because they had no real span of control. That is to say, they only supervised one or possibly two other people and very often repeated or duplicated the work of the one or two people they were supervising.

With span of control, one of the key elements is the number of people that are supervised. Opinions vary, but depending upon the circumstances, I favor a span of control somewhere between six and ten people.

Factors which need to be considered in determining span of control include the scope of responsibility of each individual or division reporting, the nature of the work conducted by the reporting individuals, the type of control systems available to the manager exercising the control and the nature of the product or service supplied by the organization.

There are numerous other factors which may come into play with these few factors mentioned only serving to illustrate that there is nothing black or white in management.

The most important aspect of using the principles of span of control and restructuring the organization, is the focus on eliminating duplication by a process of clear job definition and determining appropriate levels of responsibility by clear and complete definitions of job value.

With restructuring to determine optimum spans of control, job descriptions to eliminate any duplication and job grading to properly determine job value, organizations can address the issue of their effectiveness knowing that the efficiency of their management structure should give them a very solid base from which to work.

Succeed with a business to suit your style

In a very recent session with a close friend and client, I found myself delving into the more intricate aspects of buying a business that would bring personal enjoyment as well as a handsome profit.

Defining the profit part is usually pretty easy, because it is all about the dispassionate, unsentimental and technical aspects of business. Getting the profit is, of course, much more personal and more related to the people factors of management, but the enjoyment aspect is still more complex.

Having fun in business is a real challenge, with so many people rationalizing not making money by saying they are having fun and people who are miserable saying that at least they are making money. In my view, if you are going to take the enormous responsibility of self management and survival, you should factor a lot of fun into the self employment equation. It is very achievable and takes just a little more introspection and perhaps a useful drop of selfishness.

In looking into any business, be <u>very</u> realistic about your strengths and weaknesses and your likes and dislikes. Do not think your personality is going to change and that your skills will improve just because you own the business and have all the responsibility. Probably, the reverse will be true and all your worst characteristics will be exaggerated.

If you like having fun, get involved in a fun business in the entertainment or hospitality areas. If you like being caring and serious, get a people focused business where reliability, accuracy and honesty are the keys to success.

Like my friend, you need to realize that the hardest thing you do in starting a business is being ruthless at the most difficult time of all and with the person you are usually most soft on –you. You have to be absolutely ruthless in analyzing a prospective business and do not let yourself romance, fantasies and flirt with yourself about your ability. You could spend the rest of your life regretting it.

Sweat shops are back

In telling me about an implementation of 'Best Practice' recently, a senior executive made it quite clear that in his view best practice was a euphemism for reintroducing the era of cutbacks in proper maintenance, and particularly safety, that were interfering with the bottom line.

At first he said the changes had been tentative, with only slight decreases in budgets for maintenance and some suggestion that planned preventive maintenance might be too expensive and it might be more economical to just wait for things to break down.

Later in the piece, the maintenance budget was halved and there was a full return to the philosophy of: 'If it ain't broke, don't fix it'.

Simultaneously in the production area, employees were encouraged to work unsafely to make up for errors occurring because of malfunctioning equipment.

The strange twist to this entire exercise is that the new philosophy was introduced with the full cooperation and, in fact, active initiation of the employees' union representatives. Not only was an arrangement of maintenance cutbacks condoned, but numerous employees without appropriate training were hired and placed on the line in an attempt to boost productivity by getting better utilization of equipment.

All these strategies will no doubt sound familiar from many years ago, so there is no point in harping on them, but it is worth noting that Total Loss Control, a simple but very effective best practice system of the early 70's was combating similar attitudes. Where did it go? Why do we change and go backwards?

The key element in this case is the return to practices that were drummed out of existence in most reputable workplaces many years ago. Now, high profile companies are reintroducing these practices under new slogans that would suggest that they are the ultimate in efficiency and safety.

One can only wonder where all this will lead or whether in fact our quest for the safe productive working environment is truly a circular one that is never going to be successful.

Regrettably, senior employees of long standing appear powerless to reverse these trends. Hopefully, commonsense will prevail over time in sufficient areas to turn the tide.

Technical skill is there

Two really enjoyable incidents occurred on the same day recently.

First, I had the opportunity to interview a number of university engineering graduates and I was most impressed by their innovative approach to their profession. They really were looking forward to making a positive and inventive contribution to work within their area of expertise.

Second, a friend called by to say that he was leaving on a one year trip around Australia in a mobile home that he had bought second hand.

As we looked at his final set-up for the mobile home, I was amazed at the number of totally new technical products he had purpose-built into the mobile home. He is an electronics whiz, so doing things that are new and at the leading edge of technology is commonplace for him. However, seeing his skill applied in such a commercially applicable way was very exciting.

Also, exactly a week earlier, I had spoken to a group of engineers at the Unemployed Engineers' Support Group. This group met regularly to talk about job seeking strategies, the job market and common problems they were having as a result of being unemployed.

The subject of the seminar on this day was: 'Where is the Work?'. One of the main thrusts of my presentation was the capacity of engineers to create value with their technical skills.

Coincidentally, on the way to the meeting I had been listening to a program advertising an Inventors Expo.

I was amazed to hear that Australians had been responsible for some of the most significant inventions in world history, including refrigeration.

Meeting the array of technically skilled people that I do on a regular basis leaves no doubt in my mind that we have an extremely valuable resource.

Business owners and managers have both the opportunity and the responsibility to add value to their business and the Australian economy by using these resources.

So, where are the opportunities for these people? It certainly seems that there are some good things happening in Australia, but for each small innovative activity being undertaken, there is a much larger removal of our manufacturing or creative base offshore through lack of support.

It has certainly been my experience that many great Australian inventions and innovative thinkers have left our shores to be recognized elsewhere. Perhaps in the past it could be said that communications made it essential that they move to the focal point of their particular discipline, but these days there seems to be no excuse for failing to support these people on our home territory.

It will be interesting to see just how long we will tolerate a situation where occasional splashes of brilliance are accepted as enough, when an absolute tidal wave of the technical talent in this country could be stimulated by appropriate taxation and investment policy.

That style issue again

What is style in business and how does it relate to profit?

I was entering a bank branch recently and was somewhat taken aback by the six foot six tall, and what looked like six foot wide, security guard, smiling broadly and opening the door for me.

As I conducted my business in the bank, I noticed he provided a similar service for all customers who entered and exited the bank. He was much more like a Concierge than a security guard. As a result of this small encounter, my image of security guards and my image of this company went sky high.

Some weeks later, I was given the opportunity once again to experience service from the bank and from the security company.

On this occasion, I encountered a security guard who was six foot tall with the only other six foot measurement being around his waist. He was leaning on a rail outside the bank with his legs crossed and one hand in his back pocket looking anything but inviting and cordial. My image of the security guard and of the company went from the heights to the depths, or as one of my friends likes to say, from Old Gold chocolates to boiled lollies.

So what does all this mean for business? Well certainly it is once again an example of the need to be persistent, insistent and consistent in your presentation of your image to the general public. Like a weak link in a chain, the rule of the lowest common denominator will get you every time.

On the other hand, stylish work behavior is like a good golf shot. It looks good, it feels good and it gets the right result. Unfortunately for many people who are not prepared to put in the effort, the requirements for stylish and successful work behavior is the same as for a good golf shot. It takes many years of study and practice to learn to do it well in the first place and if you do not keep practicing and applying the skills it soon disappears.

Quality work performance requires real commitment. Fortunately, quality work is both intrinsically and extrinsically rewarding so that good training and leadership can bring about sustained high quality performance on a cooperative basis.

One very good strategy for producing stylish and successful work behavior is mentoring. Basically this involves having a person who provides a suitable role model for other people within the organization. It may be a very informal relationship or it may be more formal from a training point of view. The most important issue is that people who have the best skills are identified as being responsible for nurturing those skills in others.

Obviously, the major mentor in any organization is the Chief Executive. Unfortunately many Chief Executives are unaware of this part of their role and do not live up to the standard that is required to create an excellent organization.

All employees need to realize that they are on show on an ongoing basis. It does not matter whether you are a security guard outside a bank or a Chief Executive being observed by your employees, everything that you do has an effect on the final product that your organization produces.

So, simply put, there is good style and bad style, those organizations with more good style will do better, and that good style needs to be present at all levels of the organization.

The case of the cardboard box

There has been a continuing trend for businesses to merge and for larger businesses to develop for economies of scale in planning, creation and distribution of products and services.

Big is not always beautiful, I discovered the other day when seeking service in a chain of well known electrical stores.

This particular chain of stores has, in my experience, been a household name for quality and service for many years, and they keep themselves up to date with some fairly snappy customer oriented slogans. How disappointing then to discover that they were one of the many modern firms who didn't deliver the goods on customer service.

I entered the store carrying a rather large cardboard box containing a slippery slide I had just purchased for my four year old son. Needless to say, I was quite conspicuous.

Certainly, I was helped by a young male assistant who opened the door to let me in. I asked him, 'Do you sell CD's?'. He replied, 'Compact Disc Players or Compact Discs?'. 'Compact Discs', I confirmed. 'Just down the front of the shop', he said.

Upon approaching the front of the shop with my parcel in my arms, I spied an individual who looked promisingly like a sales assistant, standing in the front of the store speaking to a female customer while the customer's two children played nearby.

Upon getting closer, it became obvious from the conversation that the two were friends and not merely sales assistant and customer.

Thereupon, I asked if the assistant could help me find a particular CD that I wanted. He replied, 'They are just there at the front of the shop' and then made an attempt at a funny remark about what I could possibly have in this large cardboard box.

Thinking this is going to be one of those days, I carried my two meter cardboard box off amongst the CD racks and proceeded to look for the particular CD I was seeking, which I duly found.

Having found my CD, I headed back towards the assistant intent on paying my money and getting out to the car. The assistant must have known this, because suddenly his conversation intensified and he was able to completely ignore me to the point that I had to move on and approach the service desk where they processed the paperwork. I should mention, the sales assistant managed to slip in another joke about my large cardboard box as I passed by.

The two people at the service desk were a little more helpful, although they did make it very clear that I was a nuisance and tried to direct me back to the sales assistant. I promptly replied, 'I don't think he's all that interested in taking my money'.

To my surprise, the man at the service desk replied: 'It is very hard to get good staff these days'. Despite this, he still called loudly to the sales assistant, who promptly ignored him as well.

At this point, the male at the service counter turned to the female and asked her if she could assist me with the transaction. She promptly did so, but made it quite clear by her 'non plussed' expression that this was not her job.

Having had that sort of experience, people are going to conclude that I must be a glutton for punishment because I stopped at a display of vacuum cleaners. I had a need for a small powerful vacuum cleaner and these certainly looked the part.

People who are looking are a lot easier to ignore than people who are trying to actually give you money for goods they have already selected and the staff of the store totally ignored me. Ignoring me was quite a feat, because I lifted, turned, pushed, prodded, pulled and did everything I could to try to discover what the power rating was of the particular vacuum cleaner that looked as if it would meet my needs.

Yes I really must be a glutton for punishment, because I admit I did think of actually going to try to find someone to help me. Anyway, sanity prevailed and I picked up my cardboard box and my CD and I left the store.

The sales assistant must have known that I was on my way out, because at that time he came cruising down the store, made one more general remark to nobody in particular about this interesting cardboard box and headed on to do probably nothing much in particular in the sound system and television department.

This experience, after the many others I have had, leaves me to draw only one conclusion. The average Australian expects no service and so that is exactly what we get - no service.

It also leads me to conclude that the organizations who actually discover service and let people know about it, will reap a bonanza of disillusioned, disheartened and dissatisfied customers who hopefully will be able to recognize good service and the numerous benefits both tangible and intangible, that they can enjoy.

The humble business card

In a discussion in our office recently, the main subject of conversation was a crooked business card. Someone had been to a function and been given a business card by a senior manager from one of the largest, soon to be privatized, organizations in the country. This business card was unusual because it was cut crookedly both top and bottom.

So what! Big deal! Who cares as long as you can read the persons' name, their title and where they work. Is this the only function of the humble business card?

Apparently not, because the person who had received the business card and had brought it back to the office was absolutely appalled and said that he would have sent them back and would have refused to pay the bill for such shoddy work.

The immediate inference of course is that the person possessing the business card does not have the personal authority to send the business card back or does not set the personal standards that conclude that this type of work is just not acceptable. In any event, the impression was extremely negative.

The questions that arise are – 'Should we have custodians of public money who do not even know how to use their buying power to get a reasonable product?' and 'What does this mean for the eventual customers who have no control whatever over what these monopolies eventually supply?'

Clearly, the humble business card means a lot more and conveys a lot more than the name, title and address of the person. While I am sure we all sometimes wonder if the large amounts of money spent on the development of corporate logos is worthwhile, the impact of a good business card is an important part of the promotional mix.

An extra $50 spent in this area is a small investment for an upgraded image through cards that may be used for a year or more.

From a systems point of view, one cannot help but reflect again that quality assurance certification of suppliers does not guarantee that their product will be perfect and does not remove the need for the individual to be vigilant in relation to items produced for their use.

If quality certificates were this effective then every organization that appointed a Safety Officer would have no more accidents and every organization that appointed a quality manager could stop worrying about quality. Life just isn't that simple.

With all these issues, it is tempting to rationalize the situation and say that this was a mere aberration and not an indication of the overall quality of the organization. I prefer to take the more hard line attitude and say that 'what you see is what you get'.

If they accept shoddy work in something as basic as the printing of their business cards, that is a good indicator of their overall approach to quality. If a senior manager is the final recipient and user of the product, then all the more likely that other products produced for and by people in the organization with less clout will very likely be shoddy.

Finally, the reverse is not necessarily true. If an individual has a superbly designed and manufactured business card it does not mean that their organization, products and so on will be of similar quality. 'Let the buyer beware' remains the rule, but the appearance of a shoddy business card will at least let the buyer know who not to do business with.

How important are details to you? How can they contribute to your success?

_____
_____
_____
_____
_____
_____
_____
_____
_____
_____
_____
_____
_____
_____
_____
_____

TQM (Totally Questionable Management)

On a number of occasions, I have written about the simplicity and long standing awareness of the basic principles of quality management by most average workers.

Recently, more and more managers are putting forward the point of view that a lot of the hype that is being put forward under the banner of Total Quality Management or Quality Management would be better described as Totally Questionable Management.

It has been suggested that many of the principles do not accord with commonsense and in fact are a backward step compared to what has been practiced by some organizations very successfully for many years.

Some managers have raised with me the issue of whether the provision of extensive government funding for the introduction of some modern programs has in fact ruined a number of moderately successful organizations.

Change for change's sake is a well known strategy to justify ones existence in a new management role. In the smokescreen, the new manager is safe from scrutiny.

The message is clear for managers of any business. Do use your commonsense, do use your business acumen and assess very critically what is offered to you (subsidized or otherwise) in the way of management improvement strategies.

It is hard to believe that all the successes of the past have been achieved without the development of some skill.

I prefer to believe that extensive skill has been developed, but has fallen victim to the philosophy of change for change's sake and for the generation of a consulting fee.

In fact, it has been interesting to see the number of senior executives in large organizations that constantly bring up the seven year itch. Apparently they have noticed that every seven years, various organizations change from management on a product basis to management on a geographical basis or vice versa. Very often they bring in the same consultants who reverse the strategy that they installed some years before.

In my view, it is very wise to look at the performance of the organization cold bloodedly (or have someone else do it for you) before embarking on any strategy for change.

Also, any strategy for change must have specifically achievable goals against which the change strategy is measured at a particular point in time.

In the organization change area I think the philosophy of 'Look before you leap' is much more relevant than 'they who hesitate are lost'.

Training - is it any better?

There has been a great emphasis on training over recent years. With all this fuss, one would hope that there would have been major advances, at least in large firms, in the way their training is conducted.

Whilst waiting for a transaction to be completed at one of our country's largest banks recently, I had the opportunity to witness advanced training processes in action.

The situation reminded me of watching an obviously poorly trained bank teller in the inner city examine the contents of her purse on the counter while keeping me waiting on a previous occasion some years ago. I was obviously fascinated to see how far things had advanced.

You can imagine my disappointment and lack of amusement when the training process conducted at the bank counter was a classic 'how not to do it' case study. The bank officer supervising the trainee:

1. Flew through the instructions on how to conduct the transaction,
2. Was working on at least three other activities simultaneously while the trainee floundered, and
3. Walked away with her last sentence trailing in the background as the trainee tried to complete the transaction.

The fascinating aspect of this whole exercise was the trainee's commitment to trying to provide customer service and be efficient.

As the supervising bank officer walked away, the trainee shrugged his shoulders, rolled his eyes and finished the transaction as he thought was probably appropriate. Finally, he apologized for keeping me waiting.

It is sad in this whole scenario that these large organizations would have thousands of accredited trainers spending countless weeks in Train the Trainer sessions as part of a total quality management and service accreditation system.

What impact does all this have on you and me - the customer? Absolutely none at all it would seem as service at this branch has actually deteriorated over the five years that I have been going there.

Perhaps I'm just more sensitive these days to levels of customer service. No doubt companies constantly shouting quality and customer service from the rooftops must have helped make me that way.

Overall, this episode confirmed for me that we are good at addressing the veneer of so many business processes, but at the coalface where it really matters, we fail in our obligations to our employees and our customers. The only way to get around this bank's problem is to ensure that trainees are more involved in the training process, including assessing the trainer's performance.

Regrettably, true employee involvement is still much more a thing of theory than practice. Really successful organizations, however, still seem able to make the transition to new systems by genuinely embracing concepts of empowerment, quality management and customer service. It does not have to be just a public relations exercise.

Tyrants need peasants

Recently, a very sad case was presented to me by a young job applicant, who had resigned from an organization after finding a more responsible and demanding position elsewhere.

Before he left the organization, a fellow employee was complaining to him about the long hours of work (apparently till as late as three in the morning) and the generally onerous working conditions. In reply, he suggested that this person was very qualified and could also obtain a much more responsible and highly paid position without great difficulty. The co-worker made it quite clear that she was not prepared to look for a position elsewhere because she was scared of the Managing Director of the organization and how he would react.

It was the opinion of this young man, that most of the employees who continue to work at the organization in sub-standard conditions did so purely out of fear. It seems that the Managing Director was very aggressive and overbearing with all employees.

When this particular person mentioned that he was leaving to go to another organization, the Managing Director indicated that he would do everything in his power to ruin the reputation of this particular young man. In addition, when handed the resignation, he berated this particular person at length in a most insulting and demeaning way.

To his credit and good fortune, this person has a very strong personality profile and he was able to cope with this situation very well.

The unfortunate aspect of this whole situation is that the tyrant in this story needs the peasants to perform his role. If they were to revolt, come out of their shells and apply for other jobs which they would find (because of the strong demand for employees in their industry), he would be powerless.

I wonder how many people continue in jobs which they do not like and do not find rewarding, because of fear. Quite apart from the personal stress for the individuals concerned, this circumstance is bad for business in all respects. It contributes to poor futures for both the individual workers and this firm.

In the particular case, the person leaving went to a national firm with a strong reputation and a very positive employee culture. He left behind an unknown firm with a doubtful future.

In these circumstances, employees need to vote with their feet and their talent and move on to jobs that are better for them, better for the organizations that deserve to have good employees, and better for the economy.

We are all in this together

It may be old fashioned but I was still most impressed by a comment from a General Manager of a large family owned company recently.

It appears that this building supply company has been going through very difficult times.

To ease this situation, the owners, directors and senior management have taken pay cuts along with all of the rest of the staff to reduce costs and maintain the viability of the company.

As the General Manager said to me, 'We are all in this together. We have over 100 trade staff and associated support staff that we are committed to and we do not want to lose anybody'.

It is interesting to note that this is a totally opposite philosophy to the lean and mean, trim the fat, right sizing, get down to fighting weight and numerous other euphemisms for sacking people that other companies have introduced.

Certainly, if the situation became absolutely desperate, I am sure this company would introduce cutbacks. However, they did not see it as the first strategy for survival. They felt that sharing the outcome of diminished revenue and diminished profit was a much more responsible thing to do.

Perhaps if this philosophy were used on a national basis, the whole country might improve.

It has certainly been put forward theoretically on numerous occasions, but somehow the emphasis on taking the reduction in income always seems to spread to the general person in the street and in the home and not include those people who are responsible for administering the various systems of government.

Regrettably, truly selfless and sagacious political leaders are as rare as rocking horse droppings and those that do exist are so outnumbered that they must apply all their skill to survive, which is of course essential if they want to try to introduce any useful change.

In this scenario, it remains for everyone to apply the principles of survival and teamwork and share the burden in the best way they can in the various groups of which they are a member.

Whether these be employment, social groups or charitable activities, all will be feeling the brunt and sharing the load and hopefully make the burden easier. Hopefully, it will contribute to the survival of more businesses and the ultimate prosperity of more individuals.

We're 'gunna' be 'pacific'

In attending a presentation recently by a group of people who describe themselves as being from one of the leading business organizations in Australia, I was astounded at the low level of literacy.

Whilst using words such as nuance and treatise, the speaker spent the rest of the time butchering the English language. 'Going to' become 'gunna', 'specific' became 'pacific' and so on.

To add injury to insult, the presentation was essentially about quality in business management and how this organization had such a detailed and successful quality management program. As might be expected from this speaker, the slides proclaiming the efficiency of the quality management program where riddled with typographical errors.

In addition, it was fascinating to see, the three slides used were projected using extremely expensive video projection equipment. While the effect was certainly better than with a standard overhead projector, the speakers continued to speak for periods of up to ten minutes while one slide containing virtually no information remained on the screen.

This whole exercise once again goes to prove that obsession with the process combined with total lack of the awareness of the outcomes results in disaster. In this case it resulted in a bored audience who got a totally reverse impression to the one that was intended.

Overall, the presentation skills of this individual reinforced the more visible aspects of poor quality. More importantly, this aspect of this individual's presentation will continue to convey the wrong message until he is made aware of this very basic problem. Creating this awareness is not an easy task as this type of criticism is very difficult to convey successfully, particularly to a senior person with a strong ego.

It has been said that, when someone becomes aware of the problem they are more than half way towards the goal of solving the problem. In interpersonal situations dealing with personal failings, the greatest amount of tact is required and even then it is very difficult to approach these areas without prompting massive levels of ego defense. Managers general lack of skills in these areas probably contribute most to the persistent nature of performance problems that are so closely tied up with the person's ego.

Anticipating some intervention and corrective action from the manager, assumes that the manager is able to identify the problem in the first place. This may be an erroneous assumption in many cases.

All in all, there are many questions of style, skill and management training that have to be addressed in dealing with these problems. The starting point is a genuine awareness by individuals of what constitutes true quality in work performance.

With such poor perceptions of what constitutes quality in basic business communication, the road may be hard for some, but will present an opportunity for others.

What a list!

At a recent seminar I conducted, one exercise focused on the requirements of a leader. What amazed me was not the content, but the length of the list generated by each of the groups.

The expectations of today's team members of the skills and attitudes necessary to lead successfully are very high indeed.

Regrettably, the awareness among leaders and the formal training to achieve the necessary standards do not match the expectations.

Nevertheless, for those who do wish to stand out from the management crowd, the news is definitely not all bad.

There are programs provided by many organizations that fit many budgets and educational standards. They just need to be patronized to have a greater impact on the business community.

Because you do not need a license to be a leader, too many people think that you do not need any training. The end result is a lot of very lackluster leadership throughout business and industry.

If you are serious about leadership, you will do formal training at a recognized institution and you will have visible evidence (like employee ratings), that you have what it takes.

If you have not got either of these, the chances are pretty high that you are not a good leader, no matter what you might think.

If you want to find out, ask someone professional who does not fear (yes I said fear) you or losing your future business to assess how your team rates your leadership.

If you can bring yourself to believe the results (and it will be hard) it may be the most useful information your business will ever get.

Worker participation

Sometimes it is frustrating when you try in your own small way to develop new systems to allow employees to be involved and make a contribution to the success of the organization. Sadly, these frustrations do not come from the employees, who are invariably very keen, but from numerous other interested parties who would lose out if the employees' became involved and empowered.

Any frustrations I had were made to look minuscule when I read again recently about the experiences of noted Australian psychologist Fred Emery.

Emery was an outstanding Australian social scientist who did a lot of his work overseas. The pioneer of current practices in worker participation that almost everyone seems to be claiming as their creation, he seems to have experienced a lifetime of frustration.

Emery's teachings were most prominent in the courses conducted by another visionary social scientist, John Damm. As long as 25 years ago, Emery and Damm both seemed sure that the realization of the benefits of true worker participation was just around the corner.

It certainly seems now that that corner is one of the biggest on the agenda of western nations. It certainly isn't as big as peace on earth and goodwill to all, but it seems to have similar reasons for needing to be achieved and an identical lack of support.

So what does all this hair tearing and breast beating mean for business today? Simply speaking, it means that if a brilliant social scientist who committed his life to a cause had great difficulty achieving results over 50 years, business needs to be particularly committed to break down the barriers to worker participation.

One of the areas that require most attention is the building of a clear, workable relationship between the input of the individuals in the work team and the rewards they receive.

Enough work has been done on reinforcement to venture the proposal that if there is no reinforcement of positive behavior, the behavior will cease.

Too often the proposition is used that work should be rewarding in itself. This proposition is used to support the strategy that employees should contribute significantly more because it will be fun and there is no need to reward them with any type of incentive or remuneration. What a creative insult to the collective intelligence of the average employee.

On the other hand, there have been forces abroad for quite a long time which suggest that employees need to 'catch up' on past wage debts owed by employers before 'the workers' make any extra contribution. Once again, this is an institutionalized insult to the collective intelligence of the population.

Regrettably, these forces of evil or stupidity (whichever approach you prefer to take), are strongly established and it will only be when employees, managers, employers and all worker interest groups see a collective benefit, that there will be any change in this situation.

Since this community change is needed on such a wide basis, it is easy to see why Emery spent 50 frustrating years. We can only hope that it does not take total economic disaster to wake people up to what is needed.

Work with your strengths and weaknesses

It is always very hard to accept that there are certain things that we just cannot do. However, recognizing your limitations and working within them can be one of your greatest strengths.

I was working with someone the other day on some particularly sizeable challenges that had come his way. He was feeling rather daunted by them and was starting to doubt his ability to cope with the particular situations he was encountering.

As part of our discussion, I mentioned in a very makeshift fashion, the well known saying about changing what you are able to change and recognizing what it is not within your power to change. Much to my delight, I was promptly informed that this was the 'serenity prayer' of which he then gave a perfect rendition.

More importantly, being reminded of the philosophy of knowing what can be changed and what cannot be changed and having the wisdom to recognize the difference seemed to crystallize the situation that we were discussing and point the way to a solution.

It was great to be able to see someone delve into their own personal resources to cope with a problem. He had thought that he was working from a position of weakness but now realized that he had much strength that were more than adequate to deal with the situation.

Many people, when they get into a difficult situation, tend to focus on the negatives and ignore the many positives of the situation and of the strengths that would allow them to succeed rather than fail.

One of the most interesting areas in most discussions of success is how often the subject of positive visualization is included. Being able to visualize the positive side of any situation or a positive outcome of a situation is used by many personal success strategists as a technique for working through problems. One of the beauties of positive visualization is its simplicity. Mostly, it is combined with relaxation techniques to increase the effect.

From a business point of view, the most significant aspect of the positive visualization technique is as a reminder that using our strengths is predominantly about being able to focus on them. The most basic business SWOT analysis of examining strengths, weaknesses, opportunities and threats and then matching strengths to better cope with opportunities or threats, is forgotten in day to day activities.

Mini-SWOT analyses can be used at any time for even the briefest snap shot of challenges in our daily activities. This process really brings into the clear just how much resource we have to cope with those day to day problems.

So next time you have a minor crisis, use a mini-SWOT analysis to list your strengths, weaknesses, opportunities and threats. Next, make those positive outcomes clear through positive visualization. You will be surprised at how you are able to get some apparently insurmountable problems into a much more pleasant perspective. The mini-SWOT sheet on the next page is not the end of your planning. It is only the beginning. Good Luck

SWOTOS

Strengths (personal/internal)
_____
_____

Weaknesses
_____
_____

Opportunities (external)
_____
_____

Threats
_____
_____

Objectives (where I want to be)
_____
_____

Strategies (how I intend to get there)
_____
_____
_____

Conclusion

The point with so much advice is merely to make you think. This material is no different. Anything that needs to be said has been said better by someone else, but the lack of progress we all make indicates that we to keep re-visiting the message.

The aim of the Business Tips is to make comments and use examples that are topical and have some longer term implications. Changes in management practice, technology, and so on, have meant that this has not necessarily been achieved. So why publish? Well as my father used to say, anything creative is something you do for its own sake and often because you cannot help yourself.

I wanted to get these bits and pieces into a slightly more formal arrangement and I was encouraged by more than a few people as well. Finally a few close friends insisted I get this done. Yes, like the plumber with the leaky taps and the painter with the worst house in the street, I own up to being one of the many people who struggle to practice what they preach.

Probably this was what convinced me to get my stuff done. I have read just about all of the other material and it seems that anything since 1960 has made no difference to my productivity at all, so I could not recommend it to the people who were asking me for recommendations on what to read.

As my friends said, your stuff is no better than anybody else's but it's certainly no worse. A few others said your stuff is great and you need to get it out there. What is the truth? I wouldn't know. What I do know is that some readers will like it, some won't, and most won't care.

I will be happy if what I have written helps just one person. If that person is you, that is great.

Best wishes,
Karel de Laat

Teaching points

Business Success Strategies

Business Tips is supposed to stand alone, but over the years I have introduced a few basic value structures. I called these psychological frameworks in my first training sessions and then shortened this to psychoframe.

The following teaching material illustrate where I have used the psychoframe approach in business settings for goal achievement, leadership and management.

Introduction to the Basic Principles of Goal Achievement

Every idea has more to it than what is simply stated and goal achievement is no exception. However, I will try to keep the psychological mumbo jumbo to a minimum and just work with the things that are necessary to make sure you are in charge of the process.

Every time I conduct a goal achievement self-development training session, I get people to tell me what it is about their life that they have control over and could improve. I always hear the same things and most of them relate to motivation. Mostly, the people in the group have decided that they have control, but it is just too hard to change old habits.

Examples of how hard this can be are found every day in our eating habits, lack of exercise and the list goes on. What happens when someone changes those habits is what is contained in the goal achievement psychoframe. You simply decide enough is enough, set a goal and go and get it.

The goal achievement psychoframe does not focus on one area; it lets you decide what is most important to you. Actually you may decide that I do not have it covered in the values I have picked at all, which is fine by me as long as you get yourself sorted out.

What the Psychoframe does is highlight the things that are within your power to get you to where you want to be and then lets you repeat the process as often as you need.

Sayings like 'Plan the Work and Work the Plan' and 'Those who fail to plan, plan to fail' are so well known because they are so true. What the goal achievement strategies do is bring these sayings to life by letting you internalise the principles.

Keep in mind, you still need to understand and apply the principles you are using to be in charge of the process. They are simple, often well known, but only effective if you use them. So let's look at what you are using.

Goal Achievement Psychoframe

1. **Plan**
2. **Initiate**
3. **Innovate**
4. **Check**
5. **Standardise**

Basic Principles

1. Plan your approach with a strategy based on systematic pursuit of goals.

2. Initiate your goal achievement activities independently.

3. Innovate to identify strategies to maximise effectiveness.

4. Check your own performance to achieve quality.

5. Standardise your methods to maximise efficiency.

Action Reminders

- Plan to achieve specific measurable goals.
- Take action on your preferred strategy immediately.
- Innovate to succeed.
- Adopt 'right first time' as your ideal.
- Use the best system to get the best result

Action Plan

PLAN

- Set realistic goals clearly and confidently
- Plan your activities and be prepared
- Stick to the plan
- Review your progress against the plan

INITIATE

- Begin at the beginning
- Organise yourself
- Allocate and apply selected resources
- Look for immediate rewards

INNOVATE

- Always look for a better way
- Disassemble and reassemble the task/activity/process
- Relax and visualise
- Focus on the outcome

CHECK

- Accept responsibility
- Do the extra work
- Know and apply the standard.
- Own the end result

STANDARDISE

- Copy the best
- Speed it up, shorten it, organise it better
- Document the best system
- Be the best

Personal Action List (PAL)
(Key words, actions & events to memorize, visualize and discuss)

Plan

_____

_____

_____

_____

_____

Initiate

_____

_____

_____

_____

_____

Innovate

_____

_____

_____

_____

_____

Check

_____

_____

_____

_____

_____

Standardise

_____

_____

_____

_____

_____

PRACTICAL MANAGEMENT STRATEGIES

Introduction to the Basic Principles of Practical Management

After many years of conducting management programs, I came to the conclusion that there was a definite need for an approach that stripped away the unnecessary theoretical material associated with being a manager and left only the basics - the practical issues and the practical tools that are necessary to be effective.

One of the reasons for feeling that this need is so strong is the number of people that I have encountered who are trying to make an entry into the management area., but are frustrated by the 'wall of mystery'.

I believe they need to be told about techniques based on good sound management principles that are currently practiced by managers in a range of successful organizations.

The purpose of the practical management Psychoframe is to successfully convey this information and gave people the confidence to follow a simple learning path that will keep them up to date with more formal management training.

Starting the road to management confidently is particularly important point because for many people the area of .leadership and management remains one where they feel they must be constantly justifying their actions and ideas to themselves and to others. This is very unfortunate because being confident about what you are doing and being able to choose a particular method, stick with it and work towards a particular goal is integral to success in management.

It is important to know that the technique you are using is a valid and worthwhile way of approaching a problem so that other individuals cannot throw you off the track and debunk what you are doing by scoffing at you and your ideas or using some other emotive technique to try to defeat you in what you are trying to achieve.

Being totally successful as an individual, as an organization, and as an industrial society comes very much back to being well organised and astute. Being astute does not necessarily mean being highly intelligent, it means being able to marshal the resources you have, both in materials and in human effort, to arrive at a result which gives you a greater value than the combined values you started with.

Successful management means organising your resources to achieve a planned result. Sound easy, just look around to see how many major projects are late, over budget or being hit with safety infringement notices. If this all still sounds very simple, then try asking the many people who have failed to succeed in this area just how simple they found it.

The principle of top of mind awareness being essential for the belief and implementation of all Psychoframe strategies is a cornerstone of the concepts that underpin Business Tips. In other words, if you do not know and understand the principles of your management approach really thoroughly, you are much less likely to believe in what you are doing and you are much less likely to use them on a day-to-day basis. The aim is to internalise all the information and implement the strategies regularly without having to review the material and without having to think consciously about being a good leader and manager (you lead people, you manage things).

One of the most common criticisms of standard training programs has been that so much of it is forgotten and similarly so much of it is read, taken in, regurgitated and then never used. The aim of the Psychoframe system is to help stamp out the problems in leadership and management caused by people who operate on a 'Do as I say, not as I do' basis.

It is not enough know your material. You have to believe it and use it. If you do not have a philosophy that you really believe in and use, then you are not getting value from your work and probably not from your life overall.

It is important to realise that approaches like that the Practical Management Program and other psychoframe programs are basic structures for the development of personal and management skills. It is most important to realise that the purpose is the encouragement of a confident, yet analytical, approach to meeting challenges at work and in the rest of your life.

A Management Psychoframe

1. **Plan**
2. **Initiate**
3. **Inspire**
4. **Control**
5. **Sustain**

The management Psychoframe is based on the principle that most of the supervisor's or manager's time should be taken up in planning activities for others, initiating activities for others, inspiring others to perform, controlling the work of others and sustaining the work performance of others. It follows from this, that if a manager is not doing one of planning, initiating, inspiring, controlling or sustaining they are very likely performing the work themselves. That is, they are not managing.

Development of a successful Practical Management Psychoframe operates on the principle that you should be constantly alert to which of these activities you are doing so that you can clarify your performance as a manager. If you are not performing a management function while employed as a manager, you need to be alert to whether or not you are performing any worthwhile function at all. The following sections explain a little more about the nature and value of the Practical Management Psychoframe approach.

Planning

Planning activities such as goal setting, budgeting, priority setting and time management make up the group of management activities that together form the planning phase. Groups and individuals should work together towards the attainment of predetermined goals within set budgetary constraints. To do this, they need to set individual goals and objectives and practice good time management principles by establishing priorities.

Initiation

Initiating work activities for the group flows on immediately from the planning phase. Personal characteristics of drive, good time keeping, detail-mindedness and a generally innovative and sometimes opportunistic approach all contribute to suitable behaviour and constitute what is traditionally called initiative.

Inspiration

Getting work done through others requires leadership, motivation, team work and communication. These activities are central to supervisory and management activity and are not at all new. Together they combine to form the inspiration component of the manager's role where the manager inspires the group to perform the work that has been planned and initiated with them.

Controlling

Whilst such basic functions as discipline, quality assurance and the overall communication of the 'rules' of the work place fall within this area, it is important to remember that a wide range of activities contribute to the maintenance of a steady level of productive activity. Standards which are set in the Planning and Initiating and inspiration phases need to be fine-tuned in the Controlling phase.

Sustaining

Once a project has been planned, initiated and installed, the manager can take a short time to think exclusively about sustaining performance before consideration is given to the planning of the next task. This area contains most of the higher level management functions such as delegation, staff selection and appraisal, team building and the management of change. While these tasks are often interspersed with those of Planning, Initiating, Inspiring and Controlling, it is important to avoid the temptation to leave them out altogether with the excuse that there are more pressing tasks waiting. Skill in this area differentiates those who will move onto more complex management responsibilities from those who will remain at a junior level or fail as a manager.

All of **Planning, Initiating, Inspiring, Controlling** and **Sustaining** contribute to successful management. Being aware of the phases and how they contribute to the completion of the task and the development of the group's capacity to perform overall is a key element in the development of a successful management career.

Index

Personal Notes